A farm of their own . . . not big and commercialised, but a place they could lean on the gate and watch the land and animals . . .

A pipe dream? It was, until Christopher and Molly decided to emigrate from England to Canada. They were 'going west' . . . out there was land for the claiming . . .

Travelling from Toronto to Manitoba with their young children and all their possessions in a truck, they found and adopted Annabelle, the goat who joined their adventure. That journey led them to the edge of disaster and despair, but, helped by their sense of humour they carried on until at last the day came when their dreams became reality . .

Going West with Annabelle

Molly Douglas

CORGI BOOKS
A DIVISION OF TRANSWORLD PUBLISHERS LTD

GOING WEST WITH ANNABELLE
A CORGI BOOK 0 552 10621 6

Originally published in Great Britain by
Robert Hale Limited

PRINTING HISTORY
Robert Hale edition published 1976
Corgi edition published 1977

This book is set in Times 10/11 pt.

Corgi Books are published by Transworld Publishers, Ltd.,
Century House, 61–63 Uxbridge Road, Ealing,
London, W5 5SA

Made and Printed in Great Britain by
Richard Clay (The Chaucer Press), Ltd., Bungay, Suffolk.

For Christopher

CONTENTS

ONE

TAKING THE PLUNGE

What made you come to Canada? A lot of people have asked us that question. When it is twenty degrees below zero and the oil burner has run dry, we have wondered too! We have considered slick answers, such as, 'We were deported, you know,' but somehow we could never make it sound right. They might have believed us!

Leaving for another country cannot be a sudden spur-of-the-moment decision. You don't jump up and say, 'Let's go to Canada,' as if it were a drive over to see mother. In fact we worried the idea for a few years, chewed on pencils on foggy winter evenings and wondered.

What did we know about Canada? We had seen pictures of the Rocky Mountains and parts of the prairies. We knew there were the red-coated mounted police and fondly called them 'Mounties' as if we knew all about them. Some people told us that there were still wild Indians there. So what it was really like we could only imagine. Then we wondered. Would we be able to make a living in Canada? Would there be plenty of employment? We even tried listing the pros and cons (maybe cheating a little in our favour), such as:

Pros

1. We were young and healthy and had the spirit of adventure (we had once hiked across Somerset).
2. Our ambition was to own a farm and Canada had land to spare (so they told us).
3. We were not afraid to work hard, at anything if need be, to enable us to reach our goal (so we told each other).

Cons
1. We had no money (that was when we said that we would work hard at anything).
2. We didn't know anyone in Canada, such as a rich uncle we could turn to (but then, we didn't have a rich uncle in England either).

We kept finding a pro for a con. It was enough to make us hesitate.

While we were hesitating, Richard was born and eighteen months later Peter arrived. We began then to think of their future as well as our own, and we wanted a good future for them. Canada, a country always hovering at the edge of our thoughts, filled our horizon again. Canada was a young country beckoning young people. We felt its spirit of adventure and sensed its youth and we wanted adventure and youth, for all around us was age. Old England, old churches, ancient houses, tea and crumpets and antimacassars. We were coddled by the National Health and classified by the schooling system, council houses and tied cottages, all still hinting at the feudal system. This state of welfare was dulling our initiative and curbing our ambition. We were bored with class distinction. In Canada, ability would be the judge, we thought, not an Oxford accent and an old school tie. We knew some rotten cads in old school ties. In that mood we took heart and went to the immigration official at Canada House in London.

There, with the immigration official, my husband and I explored Canada on a large wall map. That official must have left Canada as a young man, for with a faraway look in his eyes he became nostalgic and told us about log cabins and the early pioneers, hot cakes, cowboys and Indians. With him we rode the West, and other directions too. We explored the Rockies, went down to the valleys, saw the forests and travelled on to the plains and prairie. We could visualize the red-coated mounted police, hitching posts, a tavern's swinging doors, cuspidors and Gabby Hayes, and there was land by the section. Land waiting there for us, just for the claiming, he added rather vaguely. He even took the cold out of winter when he told us that if there was snow, the sky was always blue and the sun very warm through glass, facing south.

We left him, full of the pioneer spirit, itching for the saddle and wide open spaces. We wanted to throw our hats in the air and shout 'Yippee Canada! Here we come.' Then we remembered, we couldn't ride a horse and how really would we find those wide open spaces?

Christopher, my husband, was born and raised on a quiet and lovely Gloucestershire farm of small meadows, where gentle cows grazed alongside docile sheep, where a stream ran cold and clear past the Cotswold stone fences and primroses nestled along the side of a winding lane.

Would I be a hardy pioneer wife? I was born and raised in the heart of London, until a bomb (on the house next door) sent us fleeing to the country (almost into Christopher's lap). I knew little about farming and cows but I did have a certificate to teach the dance; but whichever way you look at it, ballet and farming have little in common.

What Christopher and I did have in common, apart from similar likes and dislikes, was that we were both the afterthoughts of large families, left to fight our own way in the world and use what abilities we had learned and use any God-given talents we were lucky enough to have. Our parents could give us no more. They had raised our brothers and sisters and had seen two world wars and they were tired. We were almost the last straw.

Suddenly it seemed that we had to decide. Canada was beckoning, but not if we continued afraid. She didn't want us unsure and half-hearted, but willing and eager to go forth. 'We're an awful small colony to go alone to Canada,' I whispered. 'I hope the people are friendly.'

We sold the contents of our rented house, the Austin car, we paid our fare and gave the dog to a good home, then we said goodbye to our families. It wasn't easy to say goodbye. Somehow we knew we would never see them again though we talked bravely about having them out for a holiday when we were settled on our farm. They nodded and didn't look too hopeful. So we told them not to worry and I promised I would write as soon as we arrived. I mailed the first letter outside a drug store.

'Dear Mum and Dad,' I wrote at the end of the second week. I was homesick. 'We enjoyed the crossing and we weren't seasick. The boat docked at Halifax but there we saw only the inside of the customs shed. We had a long wait there but happily the Red Cross (God bless 'em) came to the rescue of mothers with young children and had a warm room for us to go with them.'

I felt like a refugee but I was thankful for the warm place to change a wet baby!

'The train took us right across Canada to Toronto. Well I thought it was right across Canada but they said there was lots more farther on. However, it was a most interesting journey, Dad.'

I didn't tell them that we couldn't afford a berth on the train and had sat up for two days in front of an Italian family enjoying garlic sausage for most of the way. Neither did I tell them how the train had wailed, loudly and mournfully, all the time. (I don't care if they are approaching roads, I say they are scaring the wild Indians away!) My letter resumed.

'As soon as we arrived the C.N.R. had farm employment for us. We are living about ten miles west of Toronto. As you see by the address it's a place called Etobicoke, and we have a nice house, Mum.'

The house was so unbelievably dirty that we scrubbed and painted for a week to make it habitable, and not only that, we were divided, by only a wall, from a family of wild Indians. Well, they were quiet at the time, but I was prepared!

'Mum! You should see all the food that you can buy in the grocery shop! They call them supermarkets over here. Butter by the pound, sugar in the sack, half a steer if you want, cut up at no extra price. I shall send you all some goodies.'

England in 1953 was still feeling the effects of war, staples continuing to be rationed, but we were children of war and we entered our first supermarket and were shocked at such abundance. We had been brought up on 'Waste not want not,' 'It's illegal to hoard,' and 'Beware black market.' We thought of all we had endured and we stared at this glut of food on every shelf and felt guilty. We bought our rations, and no more.

'Guess what I have? A washing machine. I don't know how we managed without one, and not only that, a pop-up toaster as well. We are becoming Americanized, aren't we?'

I didn't tell them that the wringer wouldn't wring and the pop-up toaster didn't pop, them both being so old, but I thought it sounded good and they wouldn't think us so mad for leaving England.

While I was getting accustomed to things Canadian, and wasting time opening all those silly little tea bags so I could 'steep the pot,' Christopher was learning how they farmed in Canada. He told me it was very much the same as in England, only you held your mouth a different way.

The dairy herd of Friesian cows were now Holsteins. The cowshed was a barn and the dairy a milk-house. He was already driving on the wrong side of the road without difficulty to fetch farm supplies such as grain (instead of corn) and alfalfa (not hay) in the truck (not the lorry)! Living within hooting distance of the trains and the highway roaring through the night, I did wonder where all that land was for the pioneering, but it was a small thought for the present, we were too busy getting used to this new way of life, and this faster pace of living. When June arrived I wrote again, for I had news for them.

'Hi folks!'

It had such a twang and sounded like the movies.

'Shucks it's hot!'

I guess that was overdoing the accent. I hadn't even heard a Canadian say 'shucks'!

'There are bluebirds and canaries and yesterday I saw a Baltimore oriole. These are bright orange birds so we feel quite tropical.'

All this was stalling for time of course, leading up to what I really had to tell them.

'The robins are three times as large as our English robin. King-size, as they say over here. Everything is king-size.'

I had bought a box of soap powder and had to keep it in the back porch—it was too large for a cupboard.

'Daddy, Mother. We have a surprise for you.'

I hoped they were sitting down.

'We have a new baby daughter! She was born on June 6th, so just missed the Queen's Coronation and a silver spoon. I wish you could see her. She weighed eight and a half pounds and is very good and content. We call her Susan Elizabeth, 'Susy' to us. Sorry we didn't tell you before and the news is so sudden, but we didn't want you to worry with our being so far away.'

The knowledge that another baby was on the way had been a surprise to us, but by then our plans were too advanced to cancel. It was too late to look back, or stay in England. We might never have been brave enough again. Also, I reasoned to Christopher, who had suddenly become apprehensive about the whole thing, 'I will hold Richard's hand. You can push Peter in his baby-chair, and this one,' I said, patting my tummy, 'we'll smuggle across.' My letter resumed again.

'We will send you a picture of the new baby.'

As soon as we can afford one.

'We have marvellous weather. It never rains all day as it does in England.'

The grass was so brown and dry I watered a patch just to remind myself.

'Susy lays outside every day under a net and she's as brown as a berry and it is even too hot for a diaper. (Mum, that's a nappy.)'

I put her on her tummy and she got a sunburn on her bottom. I forgot to turn her.

'We are all well and doing fine, so don't worry. We are saving for "our farm" though the baby's arrival cut rather a hole in our savings.'

We were broke!

We moved from one place to another twice before I felt

confident enough to write again. When our first employer, an elderly gentleman, died, his son, not keen on farming, decided to sell the estate and asked us to find employment as soon as the sale was over. Unemployment was rife, we searched for work in vain until we found the job on a vegetable farm. It was close to the town of Brampton, thirty miles away.

The house was small and stood in the farmyard (we learned after that it was used as a storage shed in winter) and the farmer was a man of few words.

'Be out in the field both of you at seven-thirty to cut spinach' were his first words. Christopher reminded him that we had a small baby. The farmer grunted. 'Then she can go behind the house and tie up the cauliflowers.'

I didn't know if this was a Canadian way of saying 'then she can go to blazes' or what, but I think he meant I had to tie up the cauliflowers. I hoped he would show me. (I didn't know they got loose!)

I need not have worried. He was at the top of the first row at seven-thirty sharp the following morning and I had to drag the baby carriage quickly through the loose soil so as not to keep him waiting. (He had reminded us pointedly that there were seven other applicants for the job.)

He gave me a bundle of strings and complained that I wasn't wearing a belt to hold them to my waist, so I used a pram-strap to mollify his impatience, and I wasn't asking him to baby-sit while I went in for a belt. He then showed me how to tuck the strings in the belt and as I approached each whole cauliflower I was to cover them with their drooping leaves and tie them around so the white 'meat' of the vegetable would keep white and unsullied.

Despite the early morning rush, coaxing the boys to eat fast and having to feed Susy, we enjoyed the fresh air once we were outside. The weather was cool and pleasant and Richard and Peter had their trucks and cars and made roads in the fine earth, while Susy slept, or gazed at passing clouds. I also found that I was quite proficient at tying cauliflowers once I had stopped holding the string between my teeth while I wrapped the head with both hands then wondered which to let go to snatch at a string!

Christopher was harvesting the spinach in another field and after that there were several acres of cabbages that he and casual labour from the town cut and crated for market, and when they were gone they cut and crated the cauliflowers. All that remained was a cemetery of white stalks, and these he cut with a disc and ploughed under.

We worked there for two months. It was seasonal work, and the work was done. We were no longer needed and we were told to go, and soon, for the house we lived in was needed for storage. The next day, in a steady rain, Christopher walked to town to find another job.

'Dear Mum and Dad, As you see, we have changed addresses. We had the opportunity of taking this interesting position twenty miles from Toronto, near a busy airport.'

It didn't matter where it was, jobs were scarce and we were lucky to have one.

'We now live in a small white frame house on a very pretty farm and also the salary is higher.'

We get all of $110 a month.

'This farmer buys and sells cattle and other livestock. Sometimes the barn is filled with cattle, pigs in the pens and calves tied to posts in the alleyways. The cows in the stalls. They are fed and the cows milked. It keeps us busy. Another day one elderly bull rattles his chain and awaits the verdict. Then we rest.'

I'm kidding, Mum. We haul out the manure and cut feed for the next lot.

'We are all healthy and brown from this Canadian sun.'

I was worried. My hands were calloused and our skin was drying like prunes.

'Susy is sitting up and trying to talk. I shall send you photographs of them all soon. Thank you for your letter, Dad. It arrived yesterday. Glad you liked the postcard. I confess, we never saw Niagara Falls. I just chanced upon the postcard. I hope you are feeling better. Yes, Dad, we don't expect it to be easy at first, and no, we haven't bought anything on the "never never".'

We never finished paying for it.

'You must have been reading about the American, and unfortunately now, the Canadian way of living. They make it all sound so easy. No, Dad. We won't look back. Yes, I think it was R. L. Stevenson who said "The best part of the goal was the journey." We have our goal in sight and are still optimistic and still think we have made a wise decision in coming to Canada.'

My words were brave but our hopes were at an ebb.

'Maybe we are showing innocence abroad for not flouting the qualifications we do have. Christopher did go to Agricultural college and he should make use of his learning but you know how he feels about this pioneering thing and having his own farm one day and not just working to draw a wage.

'Thanks, Dad, for all the good advice, and when you said that you wished you had done the same thing fifty years ago we felt, perhaps, we haven't made such a terrible mistake. Are you going on holiday? By your letter you sound as if you are going away.'

We received the cable telling us that my father had died on June 30th. I looked again at the letter. The postmark the 29th.

I was thankful that I hadn't told him that we were homeless again. That the airport was confiscating the land. The men with the theodolite had decided our fate for us this time. It was time to move on again.

TWO

WE BUY A TRUCK—
AND ANNABELLE

It was as if the gods of adversity were making sport with us. As puppets on a string we were bounced from place to place and when we were left dangling again they roared with amusement. It was enough. It was time to challenge the gods, to take arms, to oppose them, and decide our own fate for a change. But where could we go and what should we do?

We had come as brave characters in the spirit of pioneers but so far we had found nothing to pioneer and we were feeling far from brave. We told each other (for courage's sake) that we were finding the pitfalls of a strange country. 'Fools rush in', the family had warned us. No, we wanted to stay. It is a pilgrim's progress and we are fighting adversity, despair and temptation, but I secretly thought how we were moving from job to job, the dream fading a little more at every stop.

What was this Canada we had come to? A North American misfit, enviously eyeing its neighbour to the south as a sibling aping a blustering and more sophisticated brother while still feeling the ties of the mother country? A large clumsy youth of a country, wanting to grow up? Big brother beckoned while mother held him back?

Who were the Canadians, in a country that couldn't decide which flag to wave and what national anthem to sing? Was it a land of foreigners all banding tight in their own ethnic group? There was the Chinese district, the Italian, and you knew at once which was the Ukrainian part of town with their onion-top spires. All had brought their customs and traditions and kept them in a sad, pathetic kind of way and some of the people had not bothered to learn English.

Was it really a country of flashy cars, pay-later plans, gimmicks and commercials? Was all its music a sad guitar and a nasal voice? Did they really read nothing but the funny papers? Did they know nothing else to say but how hot it was, how cold it was, and Roy Rogers has a horse called Trigger?

Did all the women have harsh accents and talk only of the rising cost of food, cigarettes and of their erring husbands? Did all the men have bald heads and a paunch (because boozing was their favourite pastime), smoke large cigars and spit?

With only the radio, the newspapers and the few people we had met, were we getting a false impression? Seeing only the façade because we hadn't looked for the real Canada? We hadn't looked deep enough.

The radio blared its commercials and told me to hurry down to the supermarket for the latest bargain, even though it was eleven o'clock and a Sunday night! I was told not to miss the next thrilling episode of my favourite soap opera. Ma Perkins tried daily to placate her blundering family. I cheered her on, and she sold a lot of soap for the catchy jingle was tattooed on my brain and I went to the store singing it. 'Our Gal Sunday' was next. She was getting a divorce for sure and she was going down that collapsing mine, that li'l gal from the mining town who had married the English earl. All shades of Lady Astor, and the earl was 'a bit of a cad,' but selling more soap was all that mattered. A cornflakes box could win you a new motor boat and no one talked about the new land, they were too busy paying for the new car!

Where were the pioneers and the cowboys? Where were the Indians and the 'Redcoats'? The swinging doors? Was it all the glamour of the West and now a thing of the past?

Might as well go home, defeated as well as disillusioned. 'Mum, there are no wide open spaces.'

In England we would be sure of employment. The National Health would take care of our teeth. Yes, there would be security in the old country.

Christopher was looking out of the window. He appeared to be considering the state of the weather and if he should go fishing. It was a little unnerving in the circumstances, yet I knew that if the guiding angel was not exactly whispering in his ear, he was looking for an answer. We were held together by invisible threads of faith and trust and even if they were as taut as strained nerves they were still too strong to break.

He wanted a farm of his own in a land where he thought it was possible. He didn't want to manage someone else's farm. He wanted the problems to be his problems, the joys to be his, the disappointments too. How could we quell a dream that had brought us this far? We had followed a rainbow, and everyone had the right to a rainbow.

'Let's go West,' he said suddenly.

'That's a good idea, let's,' I agreed. 'We can't just sit here.'

Christopher left for the city. He said he was going to buy a vehicle, and while he was gone he advised me to start packing. We hadn't collected a lot of furniture so it wasn't difficult to see what we could keep and what would have to go. I sorted and packed and made a list and as I worked, Susy was at my feet and Richard and Peter were keeping lookout from a tree in the yard. Richard asked every fifteen minutes where Daddy was and what we were doing? He was only three but he appeared to sense we were an awfully small army to face Canada and be defiant!

'He's home! Here he comes!' they yelled. I heard the rattle of an approaching vehicle and ran out to see.

Christopher drove into the yard and removed himself gingerly from the seat of a half-ton panel truck (a van). It was a dusty green colour and I could faintly read the sign on the side: 'Sadowski Window Cleaners'.

'Well, what do you think of it?'

'It's fine. Does it run well?'

I didn't think it looked very fine at all. It was a dirty old van, but I didn't know what else to say and he looked as if he had been kicking tyres and looking at the inside of motors all day.

'It runs well. The motor seems good but the tyres are in a bad state.'

'There's only one seat in the front.'

'Yes. The ladder must have fitted in there.'

I looked inside. 'Oh my, it's dirty. I'll have to clean it all out, and we do need another seat if this is to be our home for a while.' Then I said hesitantly, knowing how anxious he was for my approval, 'Could you cover the sign on the side, do you think?'

He smiled. 'I guess so, if it bothers you. Anyway I have to give it a thorough going over. Don't know what to do about the tyres though.'

'How much did it cost?'

'The salesman said he was giving it away for a hundred dollars.'

'A hundred dollars? Sounds like a real steal.' I thought that was the right thing to say. I knew little of the value of old panel trucks but I knew that Christopher was attuned to the sound of the motor even if glamour had to be forsaken.

I went into the house calculating our finances, and I could do that on one hand, it was easy. We were without debts and we had exactly $200 until we bought the truck, so we now had $100. There would be the large furniture to sell. I suddenly thought how nervous Christopher must have felt at parting with half our wealth.

'There will be plenty of room in the back for the children. I think you were wise to have bought a van,' I told him when he came in. (I hoped I would be as encouraging if we were stranded in it!)

'You do?' He looked pleased. 'But it's not very elegant is it?'

'Neither was the covered waggon,' I answered.

'Well the motor didn't sound bad, and it was funny. Just driving it here, knowing it was ours, made me feel a man of property, beholden to no one, and "Master of my fate" to boot!'

Mr Brown, the farmer we had worked for, had given the children six bantam hens, and every day I went with them to gather their eggs, so we now had a good supply, and they were to prove useful. I boiled them, pickled them and put them in cakes and cookies, then sadly we killed the hens and I roasted them, all to be stowed away as provisions for our journey.

We took the large furniture to town with the stove and refrigerator, but second-hand stores weren't interested in second-hand (maybe third- or fourth-hand, they were old) goods. People preferred to buy new things, they told us. I could understand this when our radio blared daily about all the wonderful things I could buy for a small down payment and so much a month! At last a store offered a small sum for them and we took it, remembering how much we had paid for them as green Canadians.

We also had to hurry. We had promised Mr Brown that we would be gone as soon as possible. He had already departed and the men with the theodolite were practically in the garden and the bulldozers were coming closer.

Aware that we had all but given the large furniture away, we were reluctant to try and sell anything else, useful items that we had gathered during our first ten months in Canada, so we decided to buy a light trailer to pull behind the van. We searched the newspapers and all the advertisements.

We felt we were looking in vain. They were either too large or too expensive, then, just as we were wondering where we would put all the pot and pans, the hot-plate and the electric kettle, pie plates and thc hot-water bottle along with the children, we discovered what we needed outside a small garage. There was a large 'For Sale' sign attached to a sturdy little trailer, and the price was sixteen dollars.

'I think somebody cares,' I said hopefully. It was the first good thing to have happened in a long time. I quietly prayed it was meant as a good omen.

We were nearly ready. The double mattress was safe in its plastic cover and spread on the floor of the van and covered with blankets for our bedroom. Food and clothing that we needed was behind the two front seats; Christopher had made another seat and I had cushioned both of them. All other stuff was packed firmly in the trailer and covered with a canvas.

We looked around to be sure nothing was forgotten, we locked the door and hid the key where the farmer had asked us to hide it. Richard and Peter were ready behind the front seats. Susy sat on my lap.

Christopher started the motor and turned towards me. 'Well, here we go. By the way, ma, where are we going?'

'I don't rightly know, pa, but "Go West, young man".'

It wasn't a covered waggon. My bonnet didn't flap in the breeze. There were no Indians to face or dirt trail to follow, but we could shade our eyes and cry 'Westward the waggon' and whisper a prayer as faithfully as all the pioneers had done before us.

Before our journey starts I have to introduce Annabelle and to do that I have to digress a little.

One Sunday, several weeks before our departure, Mr Brown the farmer said we could take the half-ton farm truck and go for a Sunday drive. I packed a picnic lunch and we left as soon as the morning chores were done.

We wanted to see something more of Ontario so we took the Barrie Highway. The highway was wide and straight, with fir trees stretching away on either side.

We came to Lake Simcoe. We could view it far across and it appeared endless. I thought it was an ocean (only knowing ponds). We caught glimpses of sailboats and motor boats docked outside the summer cottages. We found a stretch of beach and the children paddled and we swam. For a quieter route home we took a side road, and then we saw the goats.

They were quietly browsing in a paddock, and seeing them was as exciting to me as coming upon a red double-decker bus, an English bobby, or 'the old folks' (which Christopher added).

'Goats! Let's go and pat them. It's ages since I patted a goat,' I pleaded.

After the bombing had sent us fleeing to the country (with those of my family who were not serving in the war), I had been given three small kids as a gift by a grateful farmer. The goats grew up quickly and soon there were six goats. One was a male (they also taught me the facts of life), and in no time it seemed, there was a herd of goats for me to care for. They gave us milk and butter of a rich quality, but the goats had to go.

They were comical characters with giddy prancing feet and inquisitive ways that always found them jumping down from somewhere. Once it was from the beds upstairs, that they had been happily leaping on. (Another reason why they had to go.)

To justify their playful habits they give this special kind of milk that has brought good health to many an invalid and baby. When my own babies were born I also wanted to raise them on goat's milk, but Christopher was hard to convince.

We walked along the fence and the goats ran over to us, and I then saw the sign on the gate: 'Goats and Eggs For Sale'.

'Let's go and ask about them,' I said to Christopher.

'What for? We can't keep a goat and we have plenty of eggs.'

'Oh come on. We can just be interested.'

The farmer was happy to show us his herd of Toggenburgs, Saanens and one long-eared Nubian goat.

'I have three for sale. Two young Toggs and the old Saanen,' he told us, as we patted them all and fed them from our hands and Susy kept still while they nibbled her hair (they let her pull their beards).

He told us all about his goats and he had lots to tell. Perhaps he didn't often have a chance to talk about his goats. (I am one of the few goat lovers that I know of.) I asked the price of the Saanen.

'Well . . .' he considered. 'The first thing we would want is a good home for her. She is a dear old thing and has been a heavy producer. She still is,' he said, pointing to her large udder.

Christopher quickly changed the subject to crops and weather, but before we left, we were invited to partake of a glass of goat's milk.

I smiled encouragingly as Christopher took a brimming glass full and held it like medicine, closed his eyes and swallowed, but it was cold and fresh from the refrigerator and as he wiped his mouth he did admit that it was quite good. We waved goodbye to the farmer and his wife, I with the odd feeling that we would see them and their goats again. We drove leisurely home, talking goats, and smelling of them rather as well, but it proved to be one of the best days we had spent.

Now we were in an ancient van. Going West. We were sheep who had gone astray, and would wander the wayside. In this vast and strange land, would the Good Shepherd find us, and lead us safely home?

As a mother will, I thought of our needs, and the children's well-being. I knew we had a good supply of food stowed away in boxes behind the seats and in the trailer. I also believed that children should have milk and at the back of my mind was the premise that while there was always milk for them we were not failing a responsibility and the family would keep well and strong.

I stated my case. 'The goat could go between the mattress and the back door. Then if all else fails we shall have milk for us all.'

'Hey, Dad! The milk was good. I'll feed her. I'll milk her too,' Richard offered. Peter jumped up and down and Susy joined in, not sure what they were agreeing to.

Christopher rubbed his chin. 'Well I suppose,' he said slowly. 'Seeing as we aren't sure where we are going and might end up on the Alaskan highway. . . . We'd better see if she's still for sale.'

Annabelle was standing at the fence when we arrived at the goat farm. She appeared to be waiting for us and the farmer didn't seem surprised to see us either. 'Thought you might return,' he said. 'Going on holiday?' he asked, looking at the trailer.

We didn't want to say that we weren't sure where we were going. 'Heading West,' Christopher told him. 'Mother wants to be sure of the children's milk. Is the Saanen still for sale?'

'She is, and I think she's been waiting for you. Been standing at the fence looking down the road all morning. Ten dollars okay?'

Christopher paid for her while I opened the back door. The farmer found a board to keep her apart from the mattress and he brought over an armful of straw for her bed. Annabelle came at a call and promptly jumped into the back of the truck and was hugged by three overjoyed children.

'Goodbye again,' we waved from the truck.

'Goodbye,' the farmer and his wife waved back. 'Good luck.'

THREE

OUR JOURNEY WEST

We had to detour fifty miles to re-enter the Queen Elizabeth Way. It might be a short journey by Ontario's standard of travel that could boast super-highways, over-passes, clover-leaf intersections and expressways. We weren't super-highway travellers and this four-lane freeway with tree-lined boulevard was intended for faster vehicles than our van.

The motor roared and the whole van vibrated so alarmingly that for a while I was sure we were leaving a trail of hubcaps, fenders and the contents of the trailer behind us, but the van was old and not well sprung so this was the way we would travel and after a while we didn't notice it so much, but I did notice that going as fast as we dared we barely reached the minimum speed of forty-five miles per hour.

Richard and Peter were happily resting their arms on the backs of our seats, looking ahead and full of innocent faith in us, and Susy was so sure that all was well she had crept to the back and was having a nap cuddled up to Annabelle.

'So far she's a rattling success,' Christopher said loudly above the rumble of the van. 'Is the trailer still with us?'

'Still there,' I shouted back.

The highway, straight ribbons of cement, now jerked to life with signs that appeared to shout at us. We sat up nervously and slowed down to read them, letting the impatient drivers behind us speed on by.

'This is a clover-leaf. Oh boy, and we have to find which one we take for the west-bound route,' Christopher told me. 'Quick! What did that sign say?' He looped round, caught between two cars pulling boats.

'Which sign?' I looked both sides as the flow of traffic now passed us irritably. I strained my eyes ready for the next sign as other roads branched off in intricate design.

'I haven't been on one of these things before. Quick! What did that one say?'

'Niagara Falls, and that one said South.'

'Then we have to go round again.' He looped again.

'I think we have done this loop already,' I said cheerfully. 'I never did like the maze at Hampton Court either. I think I would still be there if it hadn't been for a kind policeman,' I said, looking around vaguely for a kind policeman. 'That sign said North,' I told him helpfully.

We looped again and were on the right route eventually. Westward-bound for Hamilton, London and Sarnia and the Canadian Border to the U.S.A. where we would cross, hoping to find the real West.

Slowly recovering from the maze of loops and over-passes, Christopher said rather wistfully, 'There were no super-highways and intersections to battle with when Thomas Greely said those immortal words "Go West, Young Man".... You hitched your waggon to a star and knew there was land out there to conquer. I guess we are about fifty years too late.'

'No. I am sure there is a little left for us somewhere, but can we stop soon? I think everyone has to "go".'

Annabelle was a source of embarrassment to Christopher at first and we had to pass by several good picnic and camping stops because there were too many people. When we did find a quieter spot he carefully backed into the bushes and tethered her out of sight so that no one could see her. Yet the friendly little goat couldn't always be hidden and as we travelled on she unwittingly brought people over to pat her, and thereby made many friends for us upon the way.

Ontario was thoughtful of picnic stops and camping areas. We never travelled too far or became too weary for want of these pleasant resting areas. To us they were heaven-sent.

There was always a stone fireplace and wood cut ready for use and we first lit a fire and put on the kettle, but for this our first meal we had the cold chicken and potato salad I had ready and chocolate brownies and tea. Christopher had milked Annabelle, hiding her deeper into the bushes as he stooped to reach her udder. Susy drank it fresh and warm. Richard and Peter politely said it was good milk, but could they have it hot with cocoa in it, and we stirred it quickly into our tea.

We travelled on, staying on the tourist's route. Past the ice-cream parlours offering sixty-seven flavours or chocolate-dipped, past hot-dog stands with a neon-lighted frankfurter on a giant bun luring the hungry motorist with their odours. The boys thumped us on the back reminding us that they were hungry again and the No-Vacancy sign already flashing outside the motels reminded us to look for another camping area before they were all full.

It was dusk when we found a provincial camp site. They didn't charge admission and we pulled in thankfully. We lit the fire and I poured the rest of the milk from the jar into the saucepan for hot chocolate. I slept in the van with the children while Christopher improvised a rough shelter with the trailer canvas and after tired goodnights he crawled into the sleeping bag.

We must have slept soundly and I thought I was the first one awake. I saw daylight and wondered why I was smelling damp grass and car fumes, then I remembered we were going West, so I wished I could sleep again and wake up at home, wherever home was; but I was optimistic, so far it hadn't been so bad. I climbed over the sleeping children and found Christopher was up. He had a fire going and the kettle on and he was shaving by the rearview mirror.

I looked at the canvas and the rumpled sleeping bag and grinned at him. 'Sleep okay?' He studied his face in the mirror.

'I slept fine,' he said. 'Annabelle lay by my side all night breathing down my neck. Once I thought it was you.'

'Thank you, dear.'

'Yes, I asked her if she ever cut her toe nails or cleaned

her teeth and she nibbled my neck. Friendly creatures, goats.'

I ignored that and went to the boxes to see about breakfast maa-maaing like Annabelle. I would keep a stiff upper lip. 'Don't look back. It's the journey not the goal that is remembered. A sense of humour will see you through the rough spots. Remember how we found things to laugh at during the war. Keep smiling.'

I thought of Dad's last letter, but the journey had just begun. I hoped we wouldn't let him down.

Christopher milked Annabelle while I made porridge and we had plenty of fresh milk. We also made toast. It was smoky but enjoyable made over the embers of the wood fire. I put the crusts in Annabelle's bowl when she came to join us and her presence brought over our first visitors, mostly children, who took the boys away to play ball while we aired the van and pulled long grass for the goat to lie on. Then I dressed the children in clean clothes and washed their faces and put the clothes I had washed for them away for the next day. (If we are travelling in an old van we don't have to appear like gypsies, I told them, and brushed their hair vigorously.)

We were off, in holiday mood.

We reached London, Ontario, in good time, bypassed it, and only stopped to buy gasoline and a loaf of bread. On the road to Sarnia we had a flat tyre and changed that and used the stop to eat the sandwiches I had made at breakfast-time.

At a large garage (small ones didn't have our size tyre) we bought a used tyre, for thc sparc was worn thin. Christopher kicked it to show me. We thought all was fine until another bang had us moving cautiously to the side of the road. We changed that and ate a boiled egg each and goat's milk. At the next garage we bought only a tube and had a 'boot' put in the old tyre, wondering how far it would take us.

'A few more miles and we are in the United States of America,' Christopher called out triumphantly, and added knowingly, 'We'll buy gas in the States, it's cheaper over there.' A mile later he said, more to himself, 'Come to think of it the gallon is smaller too!'

Ahead of us were the United States flags to greet us and a notice of dire warning for people who didn't stop at the customs, lists of what we could and couldn't take into the country, and men in uniform to show they meant business.

We lined up behind sleek cars, some pulling motor boats and some pulling trailer homes. We were squeezed between looking straight ahead.

'I doubt if they will bother with us. Do we look as if we have anything to hide?' Christopher laughed.

I laughed with him. 'No, and who would guess we had a goat in the back?'

He pursed his lips and looked worried. 'I wonder what they do about goats?'

'I doubt if it's a question they have to face very often,' I said. I guess he was thinking how embarrassing it would be to have to get the goat out of the van with all these people looking on. 'Anyway, here he comes,' I whispered. The customs inspector approached the van.

'Anything to declare, folks?' He looked through the window as he spoke.

'Nothing of value, just what you see,' Christopher said nervously, wondering what the man would say about the goat in the back.

'Haven't any plants or such, eh?' We nodded and he went to the trailer and looked under the canvas. He returned to Christopher's window.

'Moving?'

'Yes. We are going out West. To Canada.'

'West eh? Wife and three kiddies?'

'Yes, Sir, that's right. Wife and three kiddies.'

'And Annabelle, daddy,' Richard piped up helpfully.

'Yes, yes,' Christopher said quickly. 'Little sister Annabelle.'

'Annabelle's my sister, daddy?'

Son, I wanted to add, last night he thought she was your mother!

The inspector gave us another glance and waved us on.

'Very well, folks. Safe journey.'

Christopher thanked him warmly and lurched forward in too much hurry causing the goat to bleat with alarm. I quickly opened my mouth as the inspector looked, hoping he would think I laughed that way.

We travelled on. We were hoping to take the ferry across Lake Michigan, into the State of Wisconsin, cutting across country into Canada once more.

We rattled through small towns, went past Saginaw City, saw corn growing, eyed the farms with wonder. Here there were no rambling farmhouses, hedges dividing fields. We didn't see hens scratching busily in farmyards or a pony waiting for the children. What we saw were orderly spaces of complex units with silver silos shining coldly against a bright blue sky.

'Giant planetariums,' I said when we first saw them.

'Silos,' Christopher told me. 'Waiting to be filled with corn when all this ripens. Strange sort of farming,' he mused. 'To us farming is a way of life, here it seems more a way of business.'

There was none of this picnic nonsense, I thought, too. 'Rest Areas,' as camping stops were now named, were infrequent and we pulled in when we did see one, thankful to find there was still the stone fireplace and wood cut ready.

While the fire was being lit I searched in boxes. There was no more chocolate cake or eggs, and the cheese was down to a slice. I thought I should keep the few other surprises for hungrier days, so I cut up the last cold chicken that was even tougher than the others had been and I brought out apples and let them have cocoa in their milk again while we sipped black coffee, admitting at last that we didn't like goat's milk stirred in it.

We were away before sunrise next day, pulling long grass for Annabelle and letting the children sleep. We wanted to reach Ludington and the ferry before noon. Travelling in the cool of day went easier and we were surprised to reach the ferry so soon. At the toll bridge Christopher hurried over to see about the crossing. He walked slowly back.

'What's the matter?'

'It costs twenty-five dollars to cross on the ferry here.'

'What's the alternative?' I asked, knowing we didn't have twenty-five dollars. He didn't reply at once. The children were awake. I dressed them and let them run out to see, with surprise, the water and large and small boats around the dock. They watched excitedly. It was a great adventure and they were happy. I was envious of their innocence and faith that all was going well and all I could think of was the money that was running short so fast. Christopher had pulled out the map, splitting now at the creases, and spread it across the hood.

'We can follow the lake here, up to Mackinac, and here take the ferry across the narrower strip.' I followed his finger as he traced the route again.

'It's a long way,' I murmured.

'Yes, a good two hundred miles, but it only costs five dollars to cross over there, I'm told.' We studied the map once more. 'I guess that's what we have to do,' he said finally.

We went on wistfully. The lake, Like Michigan, was placid and its tranquillity soothed us. We kept seeing the lake as we glanced to our left, sun-rippled through spruce and pine, and just when we thought it had left us, it appeared again, with winks of blue and at other times whole patches with a sail boat as well.

This was vacation land and we tried to pretend we were on holiday. There were 'rock shops' at the side of the road and liquor stores nestled incongruously among the pines. As we turned on the winding road we spied yachts and motorboats bobbing corkily at the dock and people in yachting caps and others carrying fishing gear but the holiday thought ended when another tyre burst with a loud explosion. The van wobbled to a stop.

'We haven't got a spare.'

'I know.'

'There was a little garage way back. I'll carry the tyre and have it repaired. We are still in the sun. Take the kids down to the water while you wait.' He mopped his head. 'Bet you could fry an egg on this tarmac.'

I led the goat and the children to where the lake rippled over the pebbles and I sat on a dry rock watching them, warning them not to venture out. Annabelle was picking at leaves and trying to keep her hooves dry at the same time, and when Christopher returned, he first bolted on the patched tyre and drove the van into the shade, then eyed the inviting water.

'I found a place where we could bathe. You go first while I find something for us to eat. Supplies are low,' I added quietly.

'I know, so is the money at the rate these tyres are going.'

After a while, refreshed from the swim, we drove on. A good tyre and another spare was our first consideration. We thought pensively what they would cost. If only we could get one our size, the size garages didn't usually have. We drove into Mackinaw City praying we would be able to find what we wanted.

Christopher was becoming a good judge of garages and at the second large lumbering one with a variety of vehicles at the back we were lucky. We changed the patched one and drove to the ferry hopefully. It was dusk but we had got this far and there was still a little money left.

We pulled down a quiet lane rather than journey on wearily looking for a camping area. We were by a green field. Annabelle had the clover's edge while we picked on chicken bones and drank milk.

Again we were away ahead of the sun and putting Lake Michigan behind us and the giant Lake Superior on our right.

The van travelled smoothly in the cool of morning and we felt safe with better tyres underneath and a spare in the trailer.

'Next stop Ironwood,' Christopher said boldly.

'All going well,' I added, crossing my fingers and whispering a prayer.

All did go well. We went through red-sand country and Indian reservations, small towns and bars that sprang from the roadside, and we drank goat's milk and only stopped for gas and oil. We reached Duluth that night, in the eye of a raging thunderstorm.

The rain drummed down on the metal roof of the van and the highway was a blur. Christopher pulled over to where he thought was the side of the road and I comforted the children while he soothed Annabelle who was bleating with fear.

When the storm had passed we drove on, glad to leave the city and find another quiet lane where we settled down for a crowded night, Annabelle included.

The morning came fresh and shining and it held promise of being another hot day so we drove off in search of a 'Rest Area' that had a fireplace and water. I was planning to wash the clothes and cook a hot meal with what I could find.

We were soon to find one. It was early and almost empty so we pulled in eagerly. Annabelle jumped out faster than the children. I was soon rinsing out shorts and tee-shirts, glad they would dry quickly in the sun, while Christopher cleaned out the van (which was smelling quite lived in). Then I studied the last of our provisions.

By careful planning we had bought very little food so far on the journey, loaves of bread and fruit was all we needed, but after this meal, my rabbit-from-the-hat tricks, in the form of chickens, cakes and cookies, slowly brought forth, would come to an end. Canada was still far away as were employment and a home. I would have to be even more frugal with the supplies.

So I cooked potatoes and made pancakes on the wood fire for I had found a half-bottle of syrup stowed away. The last of the cookies and the fruit cake I decided to keep hidden. It would be my last surprise, and I was delighted to have found the syrup. It turned out a soggy meal, washed down with goat's milk, but we all looked well on it.

Now we travelled through forest reserve, other Indian reservations and small towns, into Paul Bunyan country of legend, and we rattled into the town of Bemidji wishing we could forget about being pioneers and enjoy the sights. Being weary, we made camp early and dined on baked beans and milk, of which there was plenty, thanks to

Annabelle. She faithfully supplied us with four pints each day. Susy drank it fresh and warm (something the rest of us couldn't do) and the milk that was over we put in a jar and it kept cold in the small ice-box we had.

We were anxious now to be back in Canada, not sure how much farther the van would take us on the money we had left, where we were going to in Canada or why we were hurrying, yet Canada sounded like home, employment and a hope of better things to come.

We rumbled on. The tyres behaved, the motor coughed, then rallied, mile upon mile. Even the sign ahead was a welcome home. I read it and felt a lump in my throat. It said 'Canadian Border' and the flags were waving at us to prove it. We had got there. We were going West. I read the next sign—'Emerson Manitoba'. We laughed out loud and Christopher held my hand and the children laughed, not knowing why but because we were happy.

Our reception at the Canadian Border was non-committal. The customs inspector appeared to see nothing unusual, even waved us on with a cursory glance and a few questions as if he saw English people in vans all the time. I guess I wanted him to say 'Welcome home!'

With our eyes still to the West we were travelling a gravelled road uncertain yet where we were heading or where to stop. We made camp at another 'Picnic Ground', as they called them here, and I heard the first complaint: 'Baked beans again!' So I brought the frying pan out again and made pancakes to use up the rest of the syrup and to please them. It was another soggy supper but filling and even Annabelle lay content when Richard slipped her the bulk of his pancake and Peter offered potatoes. Susy was sitting up, her head to one side and fast asleep.

We were still heading West, facing short, sharp hills and winding roads. Christopher was listening to the sounds from the van and asked me anxiously if I too heard the knocking. More hills and turns ahead taxed the abilities of the old van and its load again and again. We held our breath, leaning forward, suffering with her. We heard with a growing apprehension the banging from under her and at the next hill we heard the splintering as she ground to a halt, her back at last broken.

Christopher opened his door and gingerly looked out. He turned to me. 'Put your foot on the brake and hold it while I wedge the back wheels,' he commanded.

There were rocks, for the road had been cut from rock. On the right was a sharp drop to rough meadowland. When the van was wedged I lifted the children out and let Annabelle loose. Left to wander, at the end of her tether as much as we were, she ran down the slope while we stared helplessly on.

Mute in our plight, we stayed with our thoughts. Could we get the van repaired, and if we could would we have enough left to pay for it? Stranded by the wayside as we were, even Canada, that we had entered so hopefully, appeared large and frightening, where no one knew us and where for us there was no one to turn to.

The sound of an approaching vehicle stirred us to action. Christopher ran ahead to warn the driver, while I gathered the children to me at the side of the narrow road. A large tractor came over the brow and on the back of it Christopher was waving. Without comment the driver turned his tractor round and hitched the van to it with a large chain. He waited while we called the goat, and looked as if he saw goats jumping into vans every day. (I liked the West already for that, an acceptance of you however odd or different.) When we were all inside he pulled us to a garage several miles back from where he had come.

At the garage he unhitched the van and drove away, waving goodbye. We didn't know his name or where he came from but we knew then we had met the Good Samaritan, and I had a feeling the Good Shepherd had sent him.

The garage was a busy one. They couldn't repair the van because they were busy with farm machinery with harvest approaching, but they knew where a back axle could be found and took Christopher down the road in a truck to get it. They gave him the back of the garage in which to do the repair. We were grateful. They left us alone and Christopher got to work.

I took Annabelle and the children for a walk to keep them out of his way but after a while we tired of walking and my arms ached from carrying Susy (who was still at the stand up and hold on stage), so I tethered the goat out of the way and we sat in the van and ate sandwiches and apples, finishing with goat's milk, passing them in turn to Christopher below.

I had to invent games to keep the children quiet. Susy soon slept but Richard and Peter wanted to be outside and when I could keep them in no longer I let them play by the van, with the spanners, old tyres and grease cans.

It was dusk when we left the garage and drove away. We had been told where the next picnic ground was located and though it was dark when we found it, we bathed the children and ourselves, removing the dirt and grease and washing their clothes. When they were sound asleep we sat by the fire's embers and thought about our situation, talking quietly. We had a tired and dilapidated old van and a trailer with its contents. We had half a bag of potatoes, some cocoa and some rice. We had an elderly goat. We hadn't any money. The repair to the van and gas and oil to get us on the road had taken the rest of that. We went to bed, too tired to worry any more. We would look at the map tomorrow we said and worry about it then.

Next morning, we decided to make Winnipeg our starting point to find work, so we turned northwards and drove on to the next town. It had a French name (Manitoba, we discovered, had these areas where people of the same or similar origin settled). We found a second-hand store, stopped outside, and looked under the canvas of the trailer. We pulled out the electric kettle and the pop-up toaster (which still didn't pop, so wasn't of much value) but they did buy us gasoline, oil, bread and peanut butter. ('It's good for you, so eat it up,' I told them, which they did, there being no other choice.)

We got to another town where we sold the hot-plate. The hot-plate took us all the way to Winnipeg where we had to buy another tyre and tube, so we sold the steam iron.

When we discovered how large and urban the city of

Winnipeg was, we felt a compulsion to go farther, away from the city to where the farms were, so we put Winnipeg behind us, venturing out on to the prairie, on a wing and a prayer, watching the gasoline gauge of our trusty old vehicle edge slowly down to 'E' and hoping it would get us as far as the next smaller town of Portage-la-Prairie, the gateway to the West (well, we nearly made it). The journey was over. We would find a home to live in, work to do, a living to make. We camped at the edge of town and waited for morning.

We were low in food, low in gas, and worst of all, low in spirits. It would be the end of the journey. We had travelled sixteen hundred miles and we were tired of travelling.

How did the early pioneers endure the long, slow journey westward? What were they looking for? Did they reach their goal? Was there joy at the end of the journey? Joy when they sighted the endless windswept prairie? Did the loneliness and desolation of what they saw frighten them, or was there just a weary thankfulness that their journey was at an end? I wondered, and that night I think I knew.

FOUR

A COTTAGE WAITS FOR US

The small prairie town of Portage-la-Prairie had one very wide main street and it was easy to see that the heart of the city was all contained down this street. I naïvely wondered, now that we were definitely West, if the people would look different? I was looking for men in cowboy hats riding by on horses.

I thought about this, parked outside the shops on the main street while Christopher went in search of employment. It was early and not many people were about, but it was as a prairie town should be, hot, dry and dusty, a bit sleepy, but I was pleased at the settled look in the old-established places of business.

Christopher was away a long time and the town was stirring. The women looked urbane enough, and no one I saw had on cowboy boots or a stetson. We were disappointed (I had told the boys we would see cowboys). Then a 'Mountie' walked by (I told the children his horse was in the stable perhaps) and he wore a stetson, and boots and even riding breeches. We knew then all was well.

I wondered if we would live near this town. Would I buy my bread at this bakery, clothes from the drapery farther down? I needed a kettle. Would I buy one from the hardware store over there? I looked with longing at the small stores.

I was tired of fleeting glimpses of the towns we had passed, where a woman wheeled her baby carriage with an air of going home to tea, of seeing groceries loaded into the backs of cars, children on swings and fathers mowing lawns, all as if they belonged. My longing was more a prayer. I was tired of belonging nowhere. I wanted to belong somewhere.

Christopher was back and Susy reached out of the window to greet him. He took her in his arms and swung her high. 'Daddy has a job, sweetheart. Everything's going to be all right.' Susy chuckled. We were all smiling. I asked him where it was.

'It's near a place called High Bluff. Have to find out where that is exactly, and somewhere for us to live.' To celebrate we all sat in the van and ate ice-cream cones, then Christopher started to drive north, away from the town. High Bluff was in that direction, he thought, and we would have to find bedding for Annabelle for there had been no long grass to pull where we had last camped.

The town soon ended, as if the prairie had a dividing line and it could encroach no farther. A field with long strips of straw and a tractor and straw-hatted driver were close by, so Christopher pulled over and went to ask him for an armful. The acreage was so vast I didn't think 'field' was the right word, no more than a lake would describe an ocean. I was wondering if the farmer managed to cut one row of oats before lunch and do another after, when Christopher was returning carrying an armful of straw. He opened the back door of the van and tucked the straw under Annabelle. He called to me, 'High Bluff is that way.' He jerked his thumb. 'Also, the fellow on the tractor said there was an empty house a few miles from here.' He jerked his thumb the other way. 'Let's go.' He set the van ahead with a roar of achievement.

He also told me that people out West never spoke of right or left turn, but east and west or whatever the direction was. The reason was, we thought, that there were few rights and lefts to turn but vast easts and wests before you got anywhere. Never being quickly sure of my east or west, I knew I would have to work at that.

He drove on willingly as dust from the gravel road billowed about us. Dust! Another problem I would have to become familiar with, but I didn't care, we were looking for a house. We all peered out through the yellow haze looking for the yellow cottage with the green shutters, as the farmer described it.

'There it is!' Christopher sighed and pulled carefully on to a grass driveway. We all jumped out but I held the children back. Perhaps it was the wrong place and someone lived there, but my fingers were crossed and my lips moved in prayer.

The yellow-framed cottage looked as if it had grown out of the prairie soil and was so simply designed a child could have drawn it, with a door in the centre, windows with green shutters each side, and a brick roof. All of it nestled in straw as grain grew around it, dwarfing the cottage even more.

I approached it like Goldilocks spying the cottage of the three bears. I knocked to make sure and then peered through the windows. Through the left-hand window I saw a tiny kitchen. There were yellow cupboards and by the window was a white table and four white chairs and against the wall was a yellow and black wood-burning stove. Through the right-hand window I saw flowered wallpaper and an armchair and through the window at the side was a bedroom and furniture.

'It's a dear little cottage. It has cupboards and a bed that our mattress will fit. It appears to be waiting for us,' I sighed.

'It's very small,' Christopher warned me. He had been peeking too. 'Do you notice there is no electricity?'

He was afraid I was too hopeful and that the cottage might not be available to us. The cramped space in the van and the feeling of homelessness was showing on both our faces.

'We could go and ask at the farm we passed half a mile back,' Christopher offered.

I didn't want to leave the cottage with the green shutters and neither did the children, romping in the straw, so we all returned to the van reluctantly. We drove down the lane to the farm and waited while Christopher went and spoke to a farmer busy oiling a large combine. We stared respectfully at the majestic implement. What was suddenly more interesting was a small boy who sprang up from the grain box on top. I don't know who was more surprised, the boy at seeing us staring at him or we at spying this Jack-in-the-box!

Richard and Peter jumped up and down excitedly hoping more boys would pop from this wonderful machine but Christopher was returning and he turned the van back to the road before he spoke.

'Yes, the cottage is for rent. We have to go to the estate agent in town to get the key. Let's leave the trailer parked outside and Annabelle guarding it, shall we, to look like our place?'

'Pete and me will keep guard, daddy,' Richard volunteered. I knew they wanted to be free of the van and playing. I hugged them. 'We shall leave the trailer but you must come with us, Richard. We don't want to lose you on the prairie.'

'Will we come back and live here?'

'Maybe. I hope so.'

We unhitched the trailer and left it close to the house and Annabelle was tethered by the tree, then we went back along the dusty road to town wondering how we could rent a cottage with no money.

We waited impatiently while Christopher went and found out about the cottage. Susy was hot and tired and the boys quarrelled. I looked up thankfully when Christopher appeared.

'The key,' he said, and held up a large rusty key big enough to open up a castle. 'The rent is thirty dollars a month, payable in advance.' I didn't reply, but we both sat wondering where we could get thirty dollars.

'We can't sell our furniture, we need it.' I told him.

'We've sold all the things that plug in,' he added.

'We've sold it all,' I cried in despair. We sat in silence, then Christopher turned to me grinning. 'No we haven't. We can sell the trailer!'

'Of course, the trailer!' I laughed out loud and the children, forgetting their discomfort, jumped up and down yelling, 'The trailer, the trailer! Sell the trailer!' We drove down the street and out of town. We were going to put the key in the lock of our front door. I felt like we were going home to tea.

The contents of the trailer were put by the front door of the cottage. I wouldn't tempt fate by arranging them. They would stay there until we were sure. Christopher took the empty trailer to town. If he sold the trailer we could live in the cottage and if there was any money left we would cook some food. IF, IF, IF—I was tired of If. I wanted a little 'for sure'.

The cottage smelled musty and unlived in and I longed to clean the windows and put a tablecloth on the kitchen table but I wouldn't, not yet, so I followed the children who had run off exploring the yard. Peter had followed Richard on fat uncertain legs, falling in the tall wheat and losing Susy who was pulling herself up again only to dump down. They yelled triumphantly when they discovered the pump by the road, hidden by long grass and stray wheat. I pumped it and Richard took over until water swished out, cold and clear. We filled a pail and then hunted for firewood, waiting for the van to appear along the gravel road.

It came, and the trailer was gone. 'I sold it,' he yelled before he stopped. 'Paid half a month's rent and bought gas and groceries. Not bad, eh?'

'Wonderful!' I ran over and hugged him, then raced ahead. I was about to set my house in order. 'The boys found the pump and lots of water,' I called back, though they had called that news ahead of me.

By evening the cottage was clean. I had found a kettle in the cupboard and now it whistled on the hob while sausages sizzled in a pan. The bunkbeds were in place and the mattress fitted our bed. The low bookcase against the wall held our books, even the curtains I had needed little alteration.

I put the tablecloth squarely on the little table and in the centre sat the wild asters that Richard had found at the wheat's edge. Then I made the tea and we all bowed our heads and thanked the Good Shepherd for having found us and led us 'safely home'.

FIVE

SETTLING DOWN

Christopher was away early the next morning to start work in the harvest field. I waved goodbye from the cottage door and looked out. It was a cool morning and a haze was lifting from the earth. I felt I was witnessing the dawn of creation and I was alone. Then I heard a whisper. It was the breeze, gently rousing the pale heads of wheat. They answered with a sigh as the breeze stole away to rustle up the barley over the road. There was nothing more to see. A few scattered bushes had tried to form a hedge and separate the wheat from the cottage yard and on the other side of the cottage were two lone elm trees. Beside it another grain crop ripened.

This was my view. I was suddenly a little frightened. What was I doing here? Blimey, me, a London girl, Cockney born and bred, alone on the prairie! Who would I talk to? I shivered slightly and heard the children waking and calling me. I went back in and put some wood on the fire.

I was soon to find out what I was doing and I was far too busy to be lonely.

The pump was about twenty yards from the cottage but there was enough water in the pail to cook porridge and make tea. I stoked the fire again and set the table. After the children were dressed and breakfast over I milked Annabelle and moved her close to the house by a bush so she could keep us in sight, for she became agitated if we weren't close by. I carried a pail of water over to her and then another for the house.

To heat the water I had to look for more firewood. When I had washed the dishes there wasn't enough water left to wash the clothes so I went to the pump again, then I had no firewood left. I was weary already and it wasn't even noon! Also I would have shaken my finger at the early pioneer woman, could I see her. 'I know why you had such large families,' I would tell her. 'You needed them to carry all that wood and water!'

The day flew by, yet I remembered to fill the lamp which was in the cupboard filled ready with coal-oil. I cleaned the lamp and glass carefully (the pioneer woman was whispering in my ear) and I was trying to straighten the wick with the scissors when Christopher arrived home.

We sat in the soft yellow glow of the lamp groping to eat a late supper. He asked me what he was eating.

'Sausages and fried potatoes, don't they look romantic by lamplight?'

He told me about his day, of hauling loads of wheat from the combine to the granary, keeping abreast of the combine without either stopping. He even remembered how many loads he had hauled.

I had been busy too, I told him, yet except for the clothes I had washed I had nothing to show for my labour.

'Don't worry, I'll saw up that limb before I leave tomorrow and on Sunday I'll have a log pile for you,' he promised.

The next day was a repetition of the day before and I had a feeling that the days after would be pretty much the same too.

The clothes I had washed had to be ironed. I knew there was an iron in the cupboard. It was that kind of cottage, equipped with all the amenities of the past. It was a complete 'do-it-yourself-kit' and as the lamp had oil the iron had its own tripod stand. I heaved them on to the table.

When I had obtained enough heat from the stove, by stoking it up and nearly fainting from the heat, I heated the sad-iron (and I couldn't think of a better name for it) on top of the stove. When I thought the iron must be hot enough I wiped it with a cloth and proceeded to iron, resting the iron on the tripod stand as I folded the clothes.

It was slow, arduous work and very warm, for the fire

had to be well stoked for the iron. As I rested my weary arm, I wondered. How did the pioneer mother find the time to bake bread, make soap, can vegetables, use a scrub board, milk the cow, and at night they said she sat at the pump organ and played 'When you come to the end of a perfect day!'

It was my fault, I knew. I just wasn't organized. I would have to get up earlier, bring the wood and water in sooner. With the baby still in diapers I would have to wash often.

The next morning I took the woodbasket and filled it ready for use. I then filled the two largest saucepans with water and put them to heat. That was instead of sitting by the first light when Christopher had left and enjoying a few moments to myself reading *Homes Beautiful*, which wasn't doing me a bit of good in the circumstances. I had found the books in the attic (when I saw the little door in the bedroom ceiling I had to find out what was up there) and read them enviously as I rubbed lard into my chapped hands.

I washed quickly and did all my work systematically, instead of stopping to pick more flowers from the ditch or standing and wondering what the black bird with the red wings was called.

I had promised the children that we would walk to the farm again, so in the afternoon I put them in clean clothes, warning them to 'keep them clean' (after all that sad-ironing). We tethered Annabelle in a fresh place, telling her we wouldn't be long, and set out to walk the half-mile to the farm.

Richard and Peter ran ahead but I was slower with Susy to carry. There was a drainage ditch each side of the gravel road and the road cut through the prairie straight as a die. We passed the wheat one side, barley the other, half as high as myself, their heads heavy on the stalks that held them, and they whispered to each other as we went by. From the farm lane two collies came to greet us, geese hissed from the side of the lane and we saw various cats. Then the boy, the Jack-in-the-box, ran to meet us.

'Hi!' he greeted us. 'I have a gopher around the back.

Want to see it?' He led the eager children away before I had reached the farmhouse.

'Is there anyone at home?' I called to him quickly.

'Sure. Mom and Donna are up with Grandma. Go in.' I went to the back porch and knocked several times.

A voice called down to me and I looked round. 'Mom and Donna are up with Grandma. Go on in and call up.' The voice came from a workshop in the farmyard. I walked through the porch and into a large kitchen; perhaps another voice would give me my next instructions.

The kitchen smelled deliciously of fresh fruit and vegetables. There was a wooden bowl of plums on the counter and jars filled close by and on the table was a boiler ready with corn on the cob. Now I heard voices from the upstairs regions.

'Grandma, come out from there.'

'Not under the bed, Grandma. Let's comb your hair.'

'Here are your teeth, Gran.'

The voices were pleading. I coughed loudly and called up a timid hello.

'Just coming!'

I waited for a few moments before the voices I had heard appeared on the stairs. The first woman was short and plump with iron-grey hair and a younger girl came behind her carrying a bowl and wearing a damp apron.

'Hello. Sorry to keep you standing there. You should have come up. Grandma was being naughty, but she's settled now. Sit down. I'll put the kettle on.'

'I must have come at an inconvenient time. I live in the yellow cottage and I was wondering...' I stood up. They were obviously busy.

They were smiling strangely at me. Mrs Wolfe, the farmer's wife, was taking an embroidered tea-cloth from the drawer.

'But we're just going to have tea, You will stay. Sit down.' She looked hurt at my reluctance. It wasn't the right thing to do obviously, but I couldn't know the customs on the prairies so soon.

Intrusion, I had to learn, was unknown on the prairies.

You couldn't, mustn't be an island. If you chose to live there you were then part of the family of folk who braved the prairies. This I gradually learned from the Wolfes.

'You came last Tuesday, didn't you?' She spread the cloth at one end of the large kitchen table. 'I was coming over. I really did have good intentions. It's Gran, you know. Being bedridden we have to be home, and what with the men on the combines now.' She looked anxiously at me.

'But I'm glad you got over,' she brightened. 'There are three kiddies, aren't there. Bob is showing them his gopher I guess. Donna,' she called, 'let's have the ice-cream from the freezer. I'll get the cones.'

We had tea from fine china with harvest cookies. 'We make them in big batches. They are spicy and have fruit in,' she told me, when I saw how good they were. 'We send them with the men's lunches when they're out in the field.'

These were pedigree seed producers. As well as the general crops grown they had experimental plots testing new seed to grow on the prairie. They were looking for heavier crops, free of disease and rust and all the other vagaries prairie crops were prone to.

These farmers were the descendants of the pioneers. It was their forebears who had opened up the prairie and had travelled the grass trail that was the road we now used, who had lived in the log houses and sod shacks while they turned the vast plains of the prairie into arable land producing the best wheat in the world. I was of course to discover many things about the Wolfes: that George Wolfe had been the world champion flax producer. The award was tucked away in a cupboard. I also learned how hard they worked while never forgetting the problems and needs of their neighbour, on the next section, or down the road. That was the unwritten law on the prairie. I learned that filling the bread baskets of the world really started in Aggie Wolfe's kitchen, where, between caring for Grandma, she made batches of harvest cookies and huge meals that the men ate in relay fashion. They worked with the weather, not letting the combines stay idle.

I sorted out the Wolfe family with Aggie's help. Bob,

now displaying his pet gopher, was seven. Jimmy, in the workshop loft, was ten years old and Margaret, the daughter, who was then away at C.G.I.T. camp (Christian Girls In Training) was twelve. Donna, the home help, lived in as did two native Indian boys who were two of many who came to live at the farm to learn new skills to find them work away from the reservation.

In time, I was to know Aggie Wolfe as an odd composite of thorough disorder with an index mind. With a vague manner she knew where everything was and what was going on. She was thrifty, as were most in this district (sections of the prairie were usually named after Scottish places or forebears). Aggie saved everything. Sometimes she wasn't sure where she hid them, but they were 'somewhere in Grandma's room'.

It was time to leave. I had gathered the children and wiped their faces clean from their ice-cream cones.

'I'll get you some eggs.' I wondered how she knew I needed eggs and that was why I had come.

'Bob found a nestful this morning. They're still fresh. I used some myself.' She brought out the basket from the back of the counter. 'We will have to find a box to put them in. Let's look in Grandma's room.'

I thought she would take me upstairs but instead we went back out to the porch where there was another door leading to a room on the right.

'This used to be Grandma's room before she had the stroke. Now I just use it for storing things,' she explained.

Boxes were stacked and articles reached to the ceiling. A collector would have cried at the treasures hidden there. I saw the china, a brief look, and the utensils that Grandma had brought over from Ireland and then there were Aggie's treasures.

'Boxes are over here,' she said, and we edged our way to reach them from on top of the wallpaper and the sealers. She brought down several to show me. 'Isn't it a pretty box? I forget what I bought in it,' she said vaguely, 'but I couldn't resist it.' She patted the box and put it back and we searched again.

'I know there are egg boxes here too. I put them inside the box I bought the boiler in. I knew it would be useful for putting the egg cartons in. Here we are.'

When the eggs were packed Aggie decided that we should also take home some ripe tomatoes and fresh carrots.

'You haven't a garden so they will be handy. Now we shall have to find a strong carrying bag with handles, then the boys can help.' She trotted back to Grandma's room and I followed her. Aggie stood at the door and took her bearings again. 'Shopping bags are over there,' she said and pointed, as if she had taken scent. 'Behind the flour barrel on top of the newspapers.'

'This barrel?' I said helpfully, looking under rolls of wallpaper.

'No, that's the sugar barrel, canning sugar. Table sugar is the tin box to the west of it. Tin boxes are handy too. I keep them all. You never know when you might need one. Here's the shopping bag, just the thing.'

We returned to the kitchen and the bag was filled with wiped tomatoes, 'or they won't keep,' Aggie informed me.

'Bring back the bag, won't you,' she called after me. 'We can use it again.'

SIX

GETTING TO KNOW OUR NEIGHBOURS

I was glad we had visited the farm. Looking from the cottage door, with no other habitation in sight. I often had the frightening feeling everyone else had left and we were alone in the world, but now I knew there was Aggie, the family and Grandma upstairs, and they were only half a mile away.

It not being our wont to rush people, we, with our typical English reserve, were prepared to be alone and inconspicuous. We still thought of ourselves as guests perhaps, in a strange house. We wanted to be welcome, so we didn't intrude unless invited. It wasn't the American way. We were learning that it wasn't the Canadian way, and it wasn't getting us anywhere either.

But we had seen the rich American tourists who had looked down their nose at British plumbing and told us how they did it back in Minneapolis. We have also (we are ashamed to say) met the Englishman who compared things Canadian with British and told them where they went wrong. We hoped not to make the same bad-mannered mistake.

So here on the prairie, our distractions would have to be of our own making, I decided. A family did make distractions. There were three lively children, and even Christopher made himself felt. He was as cumbersome as a large St Bernard in a small kennel and I kept tripping over him.

It was just a matter of attuning myself to a new way of life, I told myself. We were pretty well alone here on the prairie, surrounded and hidden by growing grain and only the odd gopher staring at us from the road on his hind legs pulling at his whiskers. Well if I was to 'Blush unseen' so it would be, like the wild asters and wild prairie rose in the wheat. I prepared to be alone, but then I hadn't discovered my other neighbours. I didn't know I had any, but they were all around me, and they knew about me.

I was busy concentrating on making bread the next day, determined to make a success of it (living among its source) when a car drove into the yard. A woman came to the cottage carrying a box.

'Hi! I heard from Aggie Wolfe that you were new in the district so I came to see how you were making out. I'm your neighbour from the south, down in the bluff there. You can see our place better when the grain is off,' she explained.

I invited her into the kitchen and she put the box on the table. 'Hope you can make use of some corn on the cob!'

'Corn on the cob. Mmmmm, we love it. Thank you.'

'What are you making?' She looked in the bowl.

I thought it looked like bread dough, now I wasn't sure. 'I'm making bread,' I said with apology. I told her of my past efforts and failure. 'It's so hard. I either forget something that should go in, or I let it get too warm, and I kill the yeast, or I get it too wet, and I have no more flour. Some of it I buried,' I confessed.

'Don't they bake bread in England?' she looked surprised.

'Oh, I'm sure they do and very well, but I didn't.'

'What did you do in England?' She looked interested.

I didn't want to say I was a ballet dancer. Sitting here on the prairie in my apron would make me look strange, too out of context. I didn't want her to think I was strange. They might not accept me. I quickly told her that my father had been an army officer and that we had at one time lived in the country and that I had been born in London. 'But we didn't bake bread.'

She shook her head sadly. I could have said I had been a famous opera star and it wouldn't have been important. What was important was my not being able to bake bread. That was a serious lack on the prairie.

She asked for a pencil and paper and wrote down a recipe that she said would never fail if I followed it. Then she left, but first she said, 'I'll probably see you at the meeting.'

I didn't know what meeting that was, but I was glad she had said it.

My days were becoming a sameness, from going for the first pail of water in the early morning to remembering to trim the wick at dusk, while all around me the harvest was being gathered. On dry days the combines worked well into the night, but not on Saturday. Then they finished early and never worked on Sunday, except for a nervous few.

Saturday evening was for going to town. This was traditional, and the stores in Portage stayed open late especially for the farmers. Christopher was home at six and he shook the oats from his hair and pockets where they had gathered and we went to town as well.

Shop lights blazed as we drove down the one wide main street (the one Portage boasted was wide enough to land a plane). Cars and farmers' trucks vied for place and we played musical chairs, driving around the block to the music from the Woolworth's store, but the parking places were taken and we lost out so Christopher found a side street to park on and we walked.

People merged along the sidewalk, some to stare in shop windows, most to look for their neighbours to stop and visit, blocking the way as we passed, and snatches of crops and weather were heard discussed. For the farmer's wife it was a respite and a welcome change from feeding hungry men at harvest-time.

The Hutterites came in from the colonies. Women in spotted babushkas and ankle-length black dresses walked behind dour men with black beards and broad black trousers and wide, black-brimmed hats. Hutterite children, small replicas of their parents, clung to their mother's skirts.

There were Indians from the reservations, leaning against public buildings, standing in tight groups as if about to make a last stand. Some of the women carried babies, not the papoose on their back as they once did but straddling their hips in careless fashion. Many looked resentful and awkward in white man's cast-off clothing and some were too drunk to care.

A pious gathering stood in a circle outside the main hotel, singing hymns and praying. This was amplified from a car-top loudspeaker and between hymns a fervent preacher waged war against sin.

There were stores that still sold over the counter and smelled of pickles and tobacco. There was a saddle shop which young bucks entered with an air of knowing what they were about, and there was a small store selling Indian handicrafts that was particularly deserted. A tall man in a clerical collar stood by the counter, hands pressed together as if praying for people to enter and buy.

The supermarket was behind the main street and there was a parking lot we could have used there. Crowds converged on the colourful store, gay as a circus with posters and balloons. It had variety and entertainment to offer to farmers who spent the rest of the week watching the crops. Next week, I thought, we would know which stores to go to, we wouldn't be strangers. When three people smiled as if they knew us and said 'Hi', we already had a small feeling of belonging.

We were gathering firewood from the back of the cottage where a fallen tree was rotting when George Wolfe called in on his way home from church. He told Christopher that a neighbour only three miles away needed a man for harvest. This was good news. The employment at High Bluff had been a journey of twenty miles a day each way. He also reminded me that the meeting was on Tuesday, that Aggie said I should be there at two and that Donna would take care of the kids.

'Are you needing firewood?' he asked. 'There is plenty in our bluff. Come and get some. The boys will help you load.'

We gathered and piled wood for the rest of the day so I was able to start the next week in good order. We had also bought another pail, making my journeys to the pump less frequent and I was better balanced. In fact I was beginning to wonder if the early pioneer woman had such a rotten life as she led us to believe! She worked hard, it is true, but it was a simple, straightforward life of manual work. She didn't have a nervous breakdown for there was nothing to make her nervous, and of course she never had the time.

There were no fuses to blow or appliances that broke down and left her frustrated and helpless until they were repaired. If the broom handle worked loose she wrapped a piece of cloth around it and twisted it in again, as I did. There was nothing that buzzed or whirred alarmingly. There was no telephone to interrupt or a vacuum cleaner's roar. There was a quiet, steady rhythm to her day, where the children's chatter didn't jar but enhanced. It blended with the birds chirping in the eaves and the rustling of a crackling fire. It was in tune with nature and peaceful. That I knew.

On Tuesday, the day of the missionary meeting, we walked to the farm directly after lunch. I warned the children that I would be leaving them with Donna and I hoped they wouldn't mind. They didn't mind, they were delighted. Donna had a speech impediment that Susy thought was baby talk and so she understood all she said. They told me not to hurry back.

'We just want to play a while. You know,' Richard explained kindly.

'Will you help Donna look after Susy if she calls you? She has her own work to do,' I told him.

'Sure thing,' he said, sounding more Canadian each day. 'We'll make out, and if anything happens to her we'll give her artificial inspiration,' he added helpfully.

Aggie was baking a cake when we got there, trotting hurriedly from the stove to the table.

'It's my turn to take lunch,' she explained.

'You'll never make it,' Donna warned.

'I have made it,' Aggie said. 'It's in the oven.'

'It's fifteen minutes to two, and the meeting starts at two. You'd better take the cookies.'

'Oh heavenly days,' Aggie muttered. 'Where does all the time go?'

'An hour of it went on the phone,' Donna reminded her. 'I'll take the cake out when it's done. Take the cookies.' We took the cookies out to the car.

'Aggie,' Donna called from the back porch door. 'You still have your apron on.'

'I'll keep it on,' she said to me. 'Donna doesn't have to know everything.'

Aggie plumped up the cushion behind her, so her feet could reach the foot pedals. Her motherly person in a white apron I thought out of place behind the wheel of the big Chrysler as we roared down the lane, sending the dogs, ducks and geese screaming out of the way. As soon as we were on the road we sped ahead, passing another car in a cloud of dust.

'Have to hog the whole road, bud,' she muttered from the side of her mouth. We turned to the right after a mile and raced down a narrow gravel trail with a low ditch each side.

'See that house on the left? The farm house,' she said, pointing to make sure I saw too.

'Yes I see it,' I said quickly, wanting to get her attention back to the road ahead.

'Uncle Rod lived there until he retired.' We swerved to avoid the ditch.

'Are you taking anyone else?' I asked.

'I offered to pick up several but they said they would rather walk. Isn't that silly of them in this hot weather?'

We turned a corner and my feet went out to imaginary brakes.

'Is it far?'

'Just a few more miles, we shouldn't be late.' I didn't think we would be either.

'Look,' she said, pointing again. 'Two combines on the go there.'

'Yes, yes, I see them,' eyes back to the road. 'They are in a hurry too.'

'I touched eighty yesterday,' she said, with a little bounce on her cushion.

'I wonder if I will,' I whispered.

'Well here we are, and everyone is ahead of us.' She pulled up by the other cars in the yard. I removed myself on shaking legs.

'Will you hold the cookies? I'll take my apron off now. I hope Donna remembers the cake in the oven.'

We entered the farmhouse as the other members were singing the opening hymn 'The Lord Is My Protector' and they continued singing softly as we went quietly to our chairs. I was handed the right page and sang thankfully, then we all sat in a circle and the meeting commenced and there on the prairie ten women worried over how they could help the hungry, homeless children of lesser countries.

We were in the home of another grain farmer and I was introduced to the district women I hadn't met before. They wanted to know what part of England I was from and how I liked living on the prairie. I answered as truthfully as I could, trying not to let on how much I was missing a washing machine and a steam iron, or an oven that went on electrically, but I couldn't entirely fool them. We were looking out of a large window of a sturdily built farmhouse at the sod shack the grandparents had pioneered in.

The floors were of polished hardwood, made, they told me, from their own trees grown by the creek. The kitchen was a mixture of colonial furniture and modern appliances. The maple rocker was close to the antique brass and black wood stove in a centrally heated kitchen. The elegant dishwasher was concealed by the maple wood cupboards.

The hostess forgave my curiosity. 'It is all so modern and comfortable compared with the past,' I breathed. I was taken to see the rest of the house, including the pump organ in the alcove and the television in the den. I saw the summer kitchen, where the windows faced the rising sun. It was large and cool for putting up preserves, cutting up the pig and feeding men at the busy time. 'You have mastered the elements.'

The hostess gave a wry smile. 'Yes, now we have it all,

and we winter in California.'

We were looking out to the garden again.

'My husband's parents started life here in that mound that was their sod shack.' I stared, marvelling at the tenacity of prairie folk.

'Your cottage would have been a mansion to them,' she said quietly. I stared at her and blushed. She had read my thoughts. She touched my arm. 'Just show this country that the struggle and the hard work can't get you down. Spit in its eye,' she said, 'and one day it's all yours.'

Annabelle was lonely. She strained at her tether and bleated softly for someone to keep her company. Her milk supply had diminished to less than a pint a day and knowing that goats need the company of their kind as much as we do, I begged Christopher to look for a companion for her. He consulted George and George said he would ask someone at church on Sunday. Church was for praying in but it was also a good time to ask for the loan of a neighbour's harrows, cake pans for a bake sale coming up, or if anyone had a goat.

There was a farmer who had a goat for sale, George Wolfe told us. He was smiling. The fact that anyone would want to keep a goat made him smile. He told us where the farmer lived. We went fifteen miles to find the farm, and the farmer grinned and tried not to sound too delighted that he had a buyer for the goat. He told us that he had bought the goat for a pet when his children were small, but the children were no longer small and neither was the goat. To make use of her he had had her bred and she was producing milk. Her name was Nanny, he said. We bought her and took Nanny home.

She was a hornless Saanen as Annabelle was, but Nanny could boast tassels and a longer beard. She produced a good amount of milk so I was able to make butter and cottage cheese again, but her udder was so low it brushed the grass and made her difficult to milk. Christopher solved the problem by building a milking stand. It was an ingenious invention with a yoke for her neck and a feeding bowl before her and a seat for me, the milk-maid, to sit on.

Annabelle liked Nanny at once. The children loved her, and she suffered a lot of patting and beard pulling. I told them not to pull her beard and that her name was Nanny, not Granny.

The days were getting cooler. The evenings were beginning to close in and I was using extra wood on the stove while the harvest was at its peak. I felt the anxiety of it as tractors and combines moved about the fields. It had become a race with the weather and we were discovering the trials and tribulations of the grain farmer.

The sun was shining as the combines prepared to harvest the swathed rows, then it rained. The sun appeared, and the grain dried, but the combine broke down at the first swath. By the time the broken part was repaired it was raining again. There had been a drought at seeding time, when rain was vital to germinate the seed. Another time there had been floods and the tractors couldn't get on the field, and that year for grain farmers there was the uncertainty of selling the crop once it was harvested.

We watched the wheat on the east side of the cottage being cut into rows of neat swaths. This was the beginning of our loaf of bread when the grain was ripe. I was glad that my bread-making was improving for such a lot of work went into that loaf of bread.

The wide blade of the swather cut the crop at the stem and the turning beaters laid it flat. The swather disappeared in the distance and returned on the next swath, until every blade was flat. When the swaths were dry, the combine arrived. It rumbled on to the prairie with the operator sitting high and important on his platform. Under him was the giant mouth and canvas tongue lapping the swath up into its giant belly. There it was chewed, digested and sorted. The kernels of grain fell into the grain bin while the straw was expelled into tidy rows behind.

The grain truck raced in, sidekick to the combine, keeping him going but awarded no credit. The truck received the grain from the combine, golden nuggets pouring from a spout, and the truck hurried back with its load for the granary. Back and forth went the truck as the combine went its slower route around until the harvest was in and the field stood stiff and blonde, the stubble like a small boy's haircut.

A few evenings later the loose straw was burned. I held tightly to Richard and Peter's hands and Susy stared from the window as we watched the rows of flame leap to the sky. I had a strange desire to dance around the flames, and so did they for they urged to be free of my hands.

Maybe it was the harvest moon, a prairie moon hanging heavy and moist. A huge cream cheese of a moon looking that it might burst around us. I shivered and took the boys into the cottage for it was cold. There was a bite of frost in the air and a breath of approaching winter.

My next important visitor was the United Church minister. He was a small Methuselah of a man. Muffled against the driving wind, he looked as if he would blow away like tumbleweed across the prairie, he was so frail. I hurried him into the house and refuelled the fire and at once he threw off his coat and scarf and bright blue eyes twinkled from a rugged weather-beaten face, then I could see he wasn't frail at all.

He welcomed us to his Church, and then over a cup of tea he told me a little of its history. The settlers of the prairie were of down-to-earth, straightforward belief. The Methodist, Presbyterian and Congregationals realized that they couldn't support three Churches so sensibly combined to be the United Church. 'That was in 1925,' he told me.

The United Church in the Macdonald district was a small wooden church of white frame, similar to others dotted on the prairie. One minister would hold services in three of these churches, living in the manse of one and journeying to the more isolated. It made his congregation very wide spread.

'Our church,' he said, 'has been attended for over seventy years. It was built by the prairie folk and has aged with them, through good times and bad. They rode the horse and cutter in the early days when the land was young and green. The cutter wheels were changed to sleigh runners in the winter, with a hot brick wrapped in a buffalo hide to keep out the cold.'

I could hear the wind howling and I stoked the fire again and wondered how this seemingly frail man had endured this rugged existence. They were 'Tough, mighty tough, in the West,' said the song. Giants in cowboy boots was how we imagined them to be. But they weren't, they were just ordinary people, blessed perhaps with a little more forbearance, wit and imagination than the rest. They pitted themselves against the elements and they conquered them. A strength of spirit was their bulwark, as were the bluffs of trees they planted and the sturdy homes they built and the help they gave a neighbour, for neighbours were important. These were their only refuge in the oft-time bleakness of the prairie.

They were gamblers too, for every year they gambled everything they had—their money, their land and their implements, and the other player was the weather. The weather was a shifty character and they never knew what he was hiding behind a cloud. Often the weather was the winner, so the farmer shrugged and said, 'there is always another year,' and when the next year came, he gambled again.

There were some who couldn't endure the waiting and wondering. The odds were too high, and they moved to town and found a steady job, but for most the will to win was too powerful. It was a mighty feeling to have beaten the weather. It was like challenging God. Yet God surely had to admire their spirit, adventuring to a desolate, seemingly God-forsaken land and still having the faith and determination to fight it, and he rewarded their faith and tempered the winds with kindness.

My gentle visitor also told me how it all started, and why the name La Verandrye was prominent, with schools and streets named for him. La Verandrye, the French explorer, was the first white man to adventure with his party along the Assinaboine River and portage the prairie. They went across bush country finding the plains of the prairie and the marsh land that led them to the new body of water they discovered. This was The Manito, for the Indians had long before heard the rushing wind through the wooded shores of the big lake telling them that their great god Manito was calling. This became known as Lake Manitoba.

These explorers found the Cree and Sioux Indians friendly, and ready to trade. Beaver, muskrat and buffalo pelts they gave the white man who in return gave them beads and shells (that was money to the Indian) and they gave them wampum, bags of salt or an axe in trade. Trading posts were then established. It was the Fort-la-Reine trading post that was to become the town of Portage-la-Prairie.

Then came the settlers: sturdy Scots from Ontario in search of better land, Icelanders from Gimli, French settlers from the St Lawrence, and the Mennonite and Hutterite brethren found colonies and a refuge there.

There was the river, the woodlots and the plains. The soil was rich and the rivers teeming with fish. Then came the advance of the Pacific Railway.

Portage-la-Prairie was settled and it grew and was now a city of 10,000 people, finding its livelihood in the industries that had developed, the government institutes that were founded, and the air force training base. It was now a busy city of a prairie nature and home to people from all parts of the world.

Still its mainstay were the farmers. They were the true founders and still stood supreme. The state of the harvest decided how the farmer would live, the car he would drive and how his children would be educated. The city looked to the farmer and the farmer looked at the weather, for the weather decided it all.

SEVEN

CHRISTMAS ON THE PRAIRIE

The cultivators covered the stubble and the trees were bare, so my scenery was changed. In the distance I could see three farms, south, east and west. If I stood on the skirting of the pump I could just see the little red school-house. Flocks of blackbirds, mourning doves and crows searched the stubble. Canada geese flew over in V-formation and I called the children excitedly when a flock of pelicans flew low enough for us to view.

Now I knew the meadowlark and the red-wing blackbird, my quiet existence gave me chance to study them. But while I was wondering what the other birds were, my neighbours were wondering what we were doing about firewood. They warned us that we would need a large amount to last us through the winter so they decided we should have a 'bee'.

A 'bee', I knew, was a 'get-together' with many causes on the prairie. The people knew that many hands made light work and a difficult or monotonous task more enjoyable. If a farmer was sick during harvest, neighbours brought their tractors and trucks to form a 'work bee'. There were 'canning bees' where they put up summer preserves in bulk, 'killing bees' for poultry raised for winter's food, and of course the time-honoured 'quilting bee'. Now the farms were modernized and there was seldom need for a 'bee' until they saw we had to have firewood. Several farmers thought it a good way to clear their bluff of dead wood and another brought the power saw, and as the wood pile of sawn logs grew mountainous several farmers' wives took turns in the kitchen and told of the days when they used wood stoves.

'I always kept my stove brush, emery paper and cloth in here,' Emily McTaggart, my neighbour to the east, told me.

'It's still there,' I told her. She brought them out and spent several reminiscent moments polishing the top of my stove. She attended the task dreamily and I thought how I often polished the warm stove top when I wanted to worry over our problems. There was something comforting about the warm stove top with the whistling kettle ready to go on for tea. 'Would you like to have those days back again?' I asked her.

'Heavens no,' she said heartily, putting the brush with the cloth wrapped around it back neatly in the corner of the warmer. 'It was hard work. Oh, how hard we worked. Carrying in the wood and water, melting snow and ice blocks in winter for the wash, making soap and grating it into the boiler, cleaning the lamps. It was work all the time. You never were done.'

'We never complained though, or very little,' Ann Ferris reminded her. 'We were content with our lot as everyone else was. We had no different problems to what the others had and I think people were more aware of each other than they are now, helping each other out when times were bad, always aware when there was trouble in our neighbour's home and being there.'

Ann's face was sad for a moment. I didn't know that a year later Christopher would help to dig her grave on a cold and snowy day, but when he did I whispered, 'Ann, we do still care.'

'But the fun we had those days,' another told me. 'Barn dances, euchre games and always the hard-times dance when we wore what we had brightened with a red patch or two.' She chuckled.

'What about box-socials?' Emily said. 'The girls did up a fancy box of lunch and they were auctioned off for a good cause and the buyer of the box had to sit and eat it with the gal who'd put it up. Some shenanigans that started, I can tell you!'

'I think that's how Pat met Mary in fact,' Ann said. 'He

built this little cottage for Mary. Oh, it looked so pretty. Mary had flowers all around it. Pat was a carpenter. They were a happy pair and he said he was going to build her a mansion one day, but he died when they had only been wed a few years.'

The wood stove had found them all remembering and the lunch was forgotten until the men walked in. They crowded in the living-room and we quickly made the coffee and finished plates of sandwiches. Then they left, leaving a stack of logs as high as the cottage for our winter fuel.

The 'bee' had brought us closer to our neighbours. We were beginning to feel a part of the community. A knock at the cottage door usually meant a neighbour, the minister or his wife or children to play with our children. So when there was a loud rapping, on the last evening of October, I was surprised to open the door to find the odd sight of a clown, a rabbit and a witch, only three feet high, and each was holding open a brown paper bag filled half full of candy and apples.

'Hello!' I was surprised at this sight. I was sure they were children despite the disguise. Was it a Canadian custom I hadn't heard of? At a greeting from the children, I took some of the candy and an apple from each bag offered and handed them to Richard, Peter and Susy, who were peeking out hopefully behind me. Say 'Thank you, boys,' I said gaily, then I asked the little people if they would come in for a while.

It was obviously the wrong thing to say, for gripping their bags tightly to them they ran away, but not without telling me what they thought of me when they were at a distance.

'How extraordinary,' I told Christopher who had come to the door. 'Did you hear what they called me? I just took the candy and. . . .'

He threw up his hands. 'Don't you know what night it is?'

I stared at him. 'I'm not sure of the date but it seemed like any day in October.'

'It's October 31st and they were out "trick or treating" on Hallowe'en night, dummy.' He was really very angry.

'Oh. Well no one told me.'

'You're supposed to know these things, and while we're about it you don't go up to people and say "Keep your pecker up, luv." Especially when they are men.'

I thought for a moment. 'You mean at the whist drive, when that fellow told me about being out of work? I was only telling him to keep his chin up, he looked so glum.'

'Then don't say "pecker". Poor guy didn't know what to do. Over here a pecker is. . . .'

'It is. . . .?'

I was still blushing as I wiped what the witches and goblins thought of me off the van.

I was told that after a snowfall there was a time called Indian summer. Nature's last warning to prepare for winter.

'Have you put your storm windows up yet?' Aggie asked me.

'What storm windows?'

'The windows in your garage.'

'Those, oh I thought they were spares, in case we broke one!'

So we put up the storm windows and latched on the storm door. What a lot of fuss, I thought. The weather is wonderful, it could be like this for weeks. The children were throwing off their sweaters and I let the fire in the stove die down at noon.

Then winter came. We awoke in early November to a white world. On soft white paws the snow had arrived and large fluffy flakes were still pattering down on the cottage roof.

'As pretty as a Christmas card,' I breathed. We all stared out of the window at the fresh carpet of snow on the yard, then I was commanded to help with jackets and rubber boots so the boys could roll in it and make snowmen and angels. I obliged, and worried about the parkas and snow boots the children didn't have.

'I hope it doesn't go away too soon,' I said naïvely, thinking of an English snowstorm that could turn to slush the next day. As if to please me it snowed again, so I melted a tub full and washed everyone's hair in the soft water. It was early November. It couldn't last, so I thought.

The snowflakes were huge. They were sent down by an expert hand gently so as not to spoil their symmetry; then jealously, a spiteful wind blew them apart so that when we ventured outside we were blinded by its darts. The wind increased until it was howling around the cottage as if daring us to leave the safe refuge of home. Each day it snowed, drifting across the prairie in waves, and when the wind dropped, as if exhausted in its anger, the snow sparkled under a canopy of blue sky. The air was crisp and it was very cold. Thus the pattern for winter was set.

We now existed, and there was a daily round of chores to make existence possible. Paths had to be cut through the snow. The first path was made to the water pump. It was the longest path. Then the pump was insulated with straw and bound with sacks. Another path was made to the goat house, the clothes line and the toilet and then a path wide enough for the van to reach the garage. Washing hung like stiff corpses and clung with a death grip to the line. I didn't know what to do with it but drag it in and wait until the house thawed it enough to hang around the stove to dry.

Farming was at a standstill and we were without an income. Even the city was quiet in winter and had nothing to offer. So we kept a nightly vigil to keep the fire burning in the stove and the house warm and I wondered what we could have to eat. In fact our simple way of life was becoming increasingly difficult. Other than the odd day of farm work, repairing machinery or cleaning grain, Christopher was without work, our savings were low and I thought of fast-approaching Christmas.

We knew we would have to use our wits if we were not to disappoint the children, for Richard was now five and excited about the coming of Christmas and presents. Peter was there and aware that something to his advantage was happening. Susy, one and a half, ever placid, always happy, caught their excitement. We couldn't let them down.

Our imagination had never been so taxed. I hunted in boxes and found enough material to make a golliwog and stuff cotton-covered animals. Christopher made a wood barn for toy animals and a cradle for a doll. We made decorations out of coloured pages of magazines and strung pop-corn dipped in red and blue dye around a lopsided tree that no one else wanted. On the top we put a star.

On Christmas Eve I coaxed them to bed after reading all the stories I knew about Christmas, from Rudolf to the birth of Jesus, and we searched the sky through the frosty window looking for the star that had led the wise men.

'Now you have to go to sleep so Father Christmas can come.'

'Who's he?'

'Father Christmas. You know. With the red suit and white beard and the reindeer and he comes down the chimney.'

'You mean Santa Claus. He doesn't do that really, you know. That's just pretend,' Richard explained.

'Okay, you little non-believer. Let's pretend. Goodnight.' I covered them up thinking how sophisticated Richard was, despite the oil lamps and a wood stove and the outside toilet.

When they were asleep we put the finishing touches to the toys we had made, trying to make them look finer than they really were. Christopher then left to see the injured cow he had helped with that morning and I iced a cake and wondered how hamburger could be made to look Christmassy, such as shaping it into the form of a turkey! There was a knock at the door and I went to see who could be calling on such a cold night.

'Just me,' said the Reverend Bowman, the United Church minister. He brushed the snow from his boots and carried in a large box. 'I don't want to waken the children, but here are a few gifts from the Church.' He put the box by the tree.

'How are you finding our Manitoba winter? Are you warm enough? I hope the cold doesn't dishearten you. It does take a little getting used to. Keep cheerful and you know our Church is always there if you need us, but I must go. Good night. A happy Christmas and God bless,' and like Santa he was gone with a nod, in a flash.

A little later, another neighbour arrived with a roast of beef, frozen and wrapped in red and green paper. Shortly after, George came with a box of sealers filled with preserves, vegetables, and chicken.

'Aggie was coming,' he explained, 'but she is looking for the gifts she has hidden away in Grandma's room and can't find. So I had best go and find Aggie. She could be lost for Christmas.'

The next knock brought a roast of pork, another brought a ham, another brought toys and fruit for the children, and with each gift was a card.

I hung the cards across the door and set the gifts under the tree. Outside I was sure the snow would be melting from the roof, at the warmth and kindness brought to us by the people of the prairie.

I went outside to meet Christopher. We stopped and looked at the stars. We thought for a moment of our families in England.

'Do they see the same stars?' I asked.

'Not now,' he said. 'It's nearly daylight there.'

'Our stars are so much bigger and brighter aren't they?'

The moon was full and almost transparent in the frosty air and stardust smothered the snow.

'Do you believe in Father Christmas?' I asked, holding his hand.

'I used to. Why, is he visiting us this year?'

'He's been. Come in and I will show you.'

EIGHT

SNOW

'Annabelle and Nanny want to have kids.' Christopher made this important announcement one day in January. He walked to the farm to phone a farmer he knew who owned a male goat. He would make an appointment for them, he said.

'He said I should bring the male here and leave him with them for a few days, for better results,' he came home and told me.

Before he left the farm, Aggie said that if he was putting a billy goat in the van he should hang a few deodorizers in there or it would smell of goat for days.

'I don't have any deodorizers,' he told her, 'and I'm not ploughing through all this snow just to get to town and get some.'

'That's all right, I have some,' Aggie told him. 'Come with me to Grandma's room and we'll look for them.'

I think Aggie had just about everything in Grandma's room, but she never liked going in there alone, as if afraid she would never find her way out.

They had to hunt for a small box that was under another box that was behind the box with the Christmas wrapping in.

Christopher started the truck, which meant warming the battery in the house and being very patient. While he was gone I made stew from the last of the gift beef and I made buns and I sewed. When he arrived home we all went to see the billy and escort him to the goat house. He had a very long white beard, or I should say yellow, and he looked as if he liked to chew tobacco and dribble a lot. He also had a pair of evil-looking beady eyes and his odour was repulsive. But he wasn't aware of his smell or his look. He entered the goat house with a lecherous leer and Annabelle and Nanny bleated timidly. I wanted to stand at the door and bar his entrance.

'Are you sure they want him in there and all that?' I asked. He was already pawing them with his sharp hooves and blowing raspberries in their ear. I knew goats carried on a strange courtship but, 'He smells horrible.'

'Aw, they love him, can't you tell? Anyway, he shouldn't smell.'

'Why not? All billys do at the mating season.'

'This one shouldn't.'

'Why?'

'He ate Aggie's deodorizers!'

At the previous missionary meeting we had all been given pieces of flannelette in different colours that we were to cut up into odd shapes and sew together to make a patchwork square, each block to be twelve by eighteen inches, then there was to be a 'quilting bee' to quilt the blocks into a comforter. The blocks were collected beforehand and sewn together and while the children stayed with Donna, Aggie and I went to join the rest of the missionary ladies for the 'bee'.

We used the large farm kitchen of an older member and the quilting frame was assembled ready. On the frame the plain back was stretched and clamped and over this was the cotton batt. 'It used to be sheep's wool we used,' they told me. 'Washed and carded.'

'Feather-soft and warm, not this stuff,' another old member sniffed.

But there were no longer the flocks of sheep they kept then, so the cotton batt had to take its place. On top of this we laid the patchwork and the three thicknesses were clamped tight, chairs were placed around and we sat down to quilt.

I was given a long, fine quilting needle and shown the stitch and we all followed the chalked directions. When our arms could reach no farther we all stood back so that the more knowledgeable ones could roll the frame sides under, pulled tightly, and the chairs were gathered closer.

We stitched and talked. I listened mostly on the periphery of this time-honoured custom, absorbing its newness.

'I did the "Dresden plate" last year so now all the girls have one.'

I waited to understand.

'"Wedding Ring" is the prettiest, I say, but it's a lot of work.'

'Well I did a "Fleur-de-lis" and two "Crazies" in a couple of weeks this winter so far and I've half-finished a "Fanny's Fan", so my family is all set up.'

Two of the older members sniffed audibly.

'Of course, when you run them up on the machine assembly-line fashion as you can with your fancy machine, Hewster, you can turn out any number. We're talking about the real thing.'

'This is the "crazy quilt" pattern that we are quilting,' another member quickly told me, drawing the conversation away from Hester. 'You see, we all sew a lot, and we can make these with all those scraps of material left over.'

'All hands to the middle, ladies,' another called.

The frame was rolled in as far as it would roll and the quilting was swiftly completed. Ruth offered to put on the binding at home using her sewing machine, so we had lunch, sitting around the enormous dining-room table, and I remained mostly a spectator as the women of the prairie chattered.

Surrounded by nothing but crops, I thought their outlook would be dull and stultified from staring out at the wheat or the snow, yet these women, offspring of pioneers, were accomplished. Teaching and nursing came naturally on the prairie when you did both in an emergency so it hadn't been difficult to take them up professionally. Sewing, cooking and homemaking were also 'learn to do or do without', and they were all expert. For pleasure they learned an instrument, helped by a parent who had learned the same way. It was all a part of growing up on the prairie.

I was sitting among a dying breed. They were proud, jealously so, of their profession as homemakers and partners in the farm.

These women didn't see the husband off to work and greet him again come evening, they saw him out of the kitchen door and followed the day's progress. If a part of the machinery fell apart, he was back at the kitchen door, and it was she who rushed it to town while he greased the other parts, for the weather was good and he had to be on the field. They didn't question their role, or complain. They were too busy, and then I realized—they hadn't once discussed the weather and snow!

'What will become of the quilt now that it is made?' I asked Aggie. We had jumped up from our lunch. It was late. We had talked too long and there were suppers to get. We struggled into heavy coats and snow boots; unplugged the car heaters, and drove the snowy trail home.

'That will be decided at the next meeting. Usually it is raffled and the money goes towards missionary work.'

When we drove into Wolfe's farmyard, Richard and Peter, who like other Canadian children loved the crisp cold, were playing outside. I went in and piled Susy into her snowsuit.

'Mom, Donna, come quick! Richard has his tongue stuck to the gate!'

I stood wondering what Bob meant while Donna rushed outside and Aggie ran to the tap.

'What happened? Where's his tongue?' I then asked, and followed Donna anxiously.

Richard was standing at the gate and his tongue was held fast to the hinge. Tears of fright rolled down his face.

'Don't pull him away!' Donna warned as I ran to him. 'Just keep very still,' she told Richard.

'He was licking the ice. I've often done it,' Bob said, in a matter-of-fact way.

Aggie came then with a jug of warm water and 'defrosted' him. Richard put his sore tongue back in his mouth and I hugged him to me, thankful that he wasn't badly hurt, and made a mental note of what to do when tongues get frozen to gates and things. It sounded like important information on the prairie!

Another snowstorm kept us indoors with the snow piling high against the snow fence by the road. We waited for the sound of the snow-plough to open up the road when it was over. We were learning about that. Wait for the storm to abate, then listen. Sometimes you could hear it clearly, other times you went to the road and looked for it to come. The sight of the plough meant you weren't trapped any longer. You could travel again.

Christopher wanted to go to town to find employment, any type of employment, for in truth we were hungry. We had lived off our gifts of meat and vegetables, using them sparingly, but without an income of any kind coming in the situation was becoming desperate, for those were the days before unemployment insurance for farm workers.

The van was under a blanket of snow and while the battery was warming in the kitchen he swept the snow away and shovelled a road out. The sky was foreboding and I hoped he wouldn't be away too long as I watched him drive slowly along the icy road. But I could always keep busy. I wouldn't sit and worry. I settled down to my quilt. In what I hoped was true pioneer fashion, I had made mittens from old sweaters, then I had made overalls for the children, using the best of Christopher's old trousers. I knew the pioneer woman would have done something clever with the jackets, but I felt I had done my best. For my quilt, I had taken all the unworn parts from blouses, skirts and dresses and I had cut them into interesting shapes. Now I was straining my eyes in the lamp light sewing them all together again.

I imagined myself the pioneer woman, bent over her needle making her 'crazy quilt'. The poor demented creature had been driven to this state of mind by all the long, silent winters, the long cold nights, endless snow and endless setbacks. There was no food in the house, for the cow had died and the crop had failed. There had also been a drought (or was it a flood?) in the 'east thirty'. It had taken a year to clear it and sow it down to a crop too!

The pioneer man was out trying to shoot a moose (or was it a buck?). Come to think of it, there must have been many lean years, for there wasn't a deer, or a moose, around, and the jack-rabbit Christopher had snared was inedible whichever way I cooked it.

Leaving Peter and Susy absorbed in play and Richard drawing on brown wrapping paper that I had to save for him, I went out to get the chores done. I milked the goats, giving them the apple peeling from the last of the apples. (I knew now what Aggie meant about being thrifty. It could mean life or death out here, I thought.) I bedded the goats well and was glad to see how thick their coats were. I then filled the wood basket and fetched a pail of water. I hurried. The wind was from the north and the snow was falling faster. I went in and shut the door, brushing snow from my head and back and wondering what we could have for supper, made with milk!

I read to the children when they were in bed later. Not that I always read to them, but more so that I could hear my voice. Perhaps I was afraid I would lose the power of speech! When they were asleep I sat idly at my quilt and heard the wind as the oil lamp spluttered.

The cottage shuddered and creaked and I got up to look out of the window but all I saw was a blank white. Carefully I opened the door a small way. To my horror the wind and snow blew frantically, as if caught together in the frenzy of a savage dance. I drew back as they swirled at me, as if they would take me in cold sinewy arms and carry me away. I pushed the door shut and I stood there and listened.

Ghostly fingers were beating at the windows in their demand to enter. Snow crept under the windows and on to the sill. It was blowing under the door and against the mat. It was even whistling to me through the keyhole!

I refuelled the fire and made sure the children were covered. The cottage had become our refuge, our only protection against the ravages of a snowstorm. Had Christopher found shelter, I wondered? Where was he, cold and lost in the snow, stranded in a frozen van unable to get home?

I listened to the howling wind and thought of the stories I had been told, frightening stories. Blizzards sometimes lasted three days. That was a true prairie blizzard. The first day it gathered momentum and into the second day, pouring out its fury; then on the third day it slowly subsided. People became lost in blizzards. They walked in endless circles until they collapsed and froze.

People were found frozen in snow-bound cars, or they abandoned their cars and tried to walk to shelter. They couldn't see, for the snow blinded them and they dropped exhausted, to be found only yards from shelter and help. This was one reason why a door was never locked on the prairie.

Then I thought of the farmer, lost on his way to the barn to tend his cattle, and of children sent home by a thoughtless teacher, later found huddled together in a snowbank.

They were often stories of the past, in the days before the snowplough kept the roads open. They were brought out when it was warm and cosy, snug and safe around a fire while the wind howled outside. Now to me they were possibilities presenting themselves quite vividly, one discarded for another more frightening.

How it all dwarfs us, I thought. However important you were, or thought you were, in the grip of a blizzard you were straws in the wind, defenceless and of no importance. You faced the rawness of it and knew how much mightier than you was the hand of nature, or was it God? I wasn't sure any more, for it even took strength to have faith against such fury.

I covered Susy who was tossing and turning, as if she sensed my worry. I put another log on the fire and set the lamp by the window, hoping it might reach the road with its glimmer. I should have stitched my quilt to keep my mind occupied. I had some knitting. I wished I had a radio. I felt so alone. Was I alone? Had the blizzard swept the rest of the world away? I paced restlessly. Finally I moved the mat from the door and looked out.

Through the curtain of snow I could make out a large

white object. I couldn't name it so I held the broom high to drive it away if necessary.

'It's me. Let me in, for God's sake,' Christopher called through frozen lips.

Lowering the broom I helped brush the snow from his clothes and he walked in on stiff legs.

When he had removed his frozen clothes and put on a warm sweater, he thawed out on hot oxo, which was all I had. It must have helped for soon his teeth stopped chattering and he relaxed by the fire. He told me how he had had to abandon the van in a snowdrift and had followed the barely visible trail home.

'Well, I have a job, so it was worth it.'

'You have? Where?'

'Gas station and hamburger stand just out of town. I start on Monday. How do you make hamburgers?'

The blizzard did last three days. On the third day it ended abruptly, as if there was no more fury to pour out. The sky was pale blue and a weak and watery sun looked down ashamed at the havoc the snow had left behind.

It had imprisoned us in the cottage and we had to force open the door and climb over the snow that had banked high against it, forming a solid wall. Christopher reminded me that the snow shovel was in the van, several miles away. He went to the farm to borrow one. The essential areas were dug first. Paths to the pump, the woodpile, the goat house and the toilet. It looked as if Mopsey, Popsey and Cottontail lived in the cottage. Last of all we opened up the driveway and looked down the snowbound road for the snowplough to open up the main artery.

Life returned to normal after the blizzard. The snowplough arrived. The thermometer quickly dipped to twenty-five degrees below zero, yet we were grateful. It couldn't snow at that mean temperature. Christopher warmed the battery and went to work each morning and we were eating again.

I decided now that something would have to be done to

make a Manitoba winter more bearable. Surely, I thought, there was more to living than this day-to-day struggle for existence, confined as we were. It just needed imagination, I told myself. There was more than struggling through snow for firewood, and cold, wet journeys to the water pump. (I always managed to spill water on myself, somehow.) I also collected snow to melt for washing. The soft water it became was benign to the clothes and what was more, it lay right by the door!

Next there was Annabelle and Nanny to milk, then feed and water. Their path was the narrowest and most awkward to navigate with two pails. Why, even going to the toilet was an adventure that had to be organized, such as, was the path open, had we remembered the toilet paper, was the journey really necessary? There was no comfort out there sitting with one's pants down against the cold north wind!

What I needed was a hobby, something to take my mind off the endless snow and cold. After the blizzard I had hidden my crazy quilt, considering I had a right to hold on to my mind a while longer. I had no desire to save boxes, or collect buttons, salt and pepper shakers or teaspoons, a popular but strange pastime I decided. So I became a 'coupon clipper'.

Magazines and newspapers were mostly passed on to us by neighbours, so when I saw 'Write your name and address here and clip along the dotted line', I couldn't fill the coupon in fast enough, and soon the mail was full of surprises. There were pamphlets on how to build your own patio, recipes for using chocolate chips, what to do with baking soda, and how to learn the guitar in seven easy lessons. There was even an interesting one on life after death. I read them all and sent for more, then the salesman called.

I saw the man drive into the yard. He wore a fur hat and large overboots. He told me he had brought the sewing machine I had sent for, and while he removed his overboots I wondered when I had done that? I had sent a lot of coupons away!

He lifted a small machine from a rather worn case. 'This

one, ma'am, is the small model, and confidentially, it's cheap.' He shook his head sadly. 'Hate to see you buy this machine. You're going to be disappointed, I know it.'

I nodded emphatically, agreeing with him. I hoped he would then go away knowing that.

'No, it's not what I want at all,' I told him.

'Ah, that's the way. Now I have the very machine for you, you'll love it,' and before I could speak he was jumping into his overboots and without buckling them he hurried to his car.

'This is it.' He was breathing heavily. He lifted the machine on to the table and took it from its shining case.

'See, all the fancy attachments, you can fine-stitch, embroider, make button-holes, go backwards and forwards. Does everything but talk, does this baby.' He laughed, and I winced.

'I'll just demonstrate. Have you a small piece of material, no, don't worry, I have a piece right here.'

Speechless I watched him unwind the cord and hold out the plug while searching for a socket. I pointed to the oil lamp. He must have thought it was a trick. He looked very annoyed, put the machine back in the case and snapped it shut.

'Have you a treadle machine?' I asked, hoping to make amends. 'No, we only sell electric,' and he hurried to his car without buckling his overboots again and drove away.

The children had been very quiet and interested during the salesman's visit but when Christopher came home they rushed to tell him about the man who came and kept taking his boots off. So I had to tell him. Then I had to promise to consider more carefully the coupon I clipped. 'And read the small print,' he roared.

Yet I toured the world via the coloured pictures and printed pages of the booklets that arrived and suffered with a bout of nostalgia on seeing the Cotswolds. Then I couldn't have any more booklets without paying for them. So I appreciated good music and 'The Old Masters' on the ancient hand-wound gramophone that Aggie had found buried in Grandma's room. I'd put myself in another world

as I listened to Concerto for Two Trumpets, by Vivaldi. I was going to listen to Toccata and Fugue in D Minor, by
broke it.
Bach, again one evening, but Christopher accidentally

Another coupon I sent away brought me other 'Old Masters' to appreciate, in the form of famous art reproductions. Then I found Richard and two other little boys staring intently at them. He brought them out when the missionary ladies called. Showing them Renoir's nudes, he said, 'Mommy keeps them under the bed and brings them out.' I sent them back. I didn't think it was yet the time or place for the 'Old Masters'.

Christopher was intent on putting a stop to all my coupon clipping for I found now when I read a magazine that there were little squares missing. He thought he was nipping (or was it clipping) it in the bud. I thought he could find something better to do than cut squares out of magazines but I took the hint. But it was after I had sent for the free yoga lessons. The cottage was too small to jeté or polka or ballet at all, so I thought yoga would be the thing. I had my head balanced on the floor in the classic yoga position, but with my chest resting against the chesterfield couch when Aggie walked in. She nodded wisely as I righted myself. 'I'm always telling Donna there is dust under the couch, if she would really look, but doesn't that make you dizzy?' she asked.

We went to a whist drive and social evening. Donna offered to stay with the children. Christopher went and brought her to the cottage in the van while I stoked the fire and put the children's pyjamas ready.

We had to take sandwiches or a cake and as soon as we arrived at the school we spread these ready on a long table. Someone else stoked the coal heater and the coffee pot was set ready while the men put up the card tables.

We didn't give the weather a thought, and it wasn't mentioned. We enjoyed ourselves. The Manitoba winter was a condition that we couldn't alter, so they built warm homes, wore warm clothing and enjoyed the vigour of the outside, and as one old-timer said, 'You won't find cold like you get here. It's special cold!'

It was as if the climate had tempered them to acquiescence and they had long ago shrugged their shoulders and took it in their stride, even enjoyed its invigoration. They smiled, and were gentle. Suddenly Canada and winter frightened us less. If these people lived well now, they too had been through the struggles of getting established, as had their forefathers. They knew all about it. What it was like to be snowbound, and how to live with it. They boasted 'cold weather' stories and how they had come through, and luckless farmers' tales. One farmer, a French Canadian, needed little urging to recite. 'The Cremation of Sam McGee'. It was his party piece.

'Now what about some music?' another suggested, when the stories had run out.

I privately wondered who could possibly be musical among this assorted assembly of farmers, of ponderous step and thoughtful cogitation.

A serious-looking, small, bald-headed man snapped his braces and reached for a violin hidden behind the piano. A farmer's wife (who played the organ at church) went primly to the piano and a younger man brought in his guitar from the cloakroom. There was a quick tune-up, the fiddler stamped his foot four times, and they played.

They had no music, they didn't need music and perhaps they couldn't have read it. Their music was born of the prairie barn dance. A part of the prairie and of them. Bred in the bone with a toe-tapping rhythm and a two-four beat. It compelled us to dance.

'We have enough for two squares. Everyone up.' We were urged forward.

'What do I do?' They were joining me to a square.

'It's easy. Just listen to the "caller".'

I looked at Christopher. He was joined to the other square and I could see by his worried face that he was hoping I would rescue him. I smiled encouragingly. A quiet farmer who had stammered when he met us now bellowed for all to hear, but his voice was musical.

'Honour your partner one and all,' he ordered. I was bowed at by my partner. I returned with a curtsy, and then to the rest. We all bowed.

'Allemande left.'

I watched my partner, who only took my hand and passed on. It was grand chain, I realized. How grander 'Allemande' sounded, I thought, and I tripped around, much too daintily I could see, so I shuffled my feet more, in what I hoped was the right way.

'Swing her up, swing her high.' My partner was taking me and pulling me off my feet. I screamed with fear. I was dizzy but no sooner had he released me than another man did the same. This wasn't dancing, it was wrestling!

'Allemande left, pass her by, wink to the other one on the sly.' I went the wrong way. My partner pulled me back.

'First couple up. Circle half inside under outside over.'

They all seemed to know what that meant but me, and I had lost my partner again. (I was glad I hadn't mentioned the ballet, I was flunking a square dance!) My partner rescued me with remarkable patience.

The 'caller' went on with instructions. 'Over here, over there, over yonder I don't care.'

I found myself in the other square. My partner dragged me back. Christopher waved. He was definitely going the wrong way. He was going outside!

'Ladies cross your lily-white hands and men your black and tan.'

We swung around as the fiddler quickened the pace, then with a last swing around my partner, the square was ended and we all breathlessly sat down. It was time to serve the lunch. We ate heartily before we all shuffled into our winter togs and went out into the cold night.

NINE

WE BEGIN TO FEEL CANADIAN

Easter was only a few weeks away yet the snow lay deeper than ever. It had gathered into hills against the snow fence along the road and the side-lanes were now tunnels where the snow-plough had pushed the snow each side.

From early November until April we had lived in this world of white. When the air was calm and the sky blue, the sunshine made my eyes smart and I had to wear sunglasses to go to the pump! When the sky was grey and the wind blew sideways, we looked for another blizzard and stayed indoors.

I couldn't remember what green grass and leaves on trees looked like. My trees were dark lines, a Chinese print on a pale canvas. I longed for a soft, gentle rain. I tried to imagine its scent, fresh, a little earthy. Earth was only seen here in clay pots. (Was that the reason the prairie people took such care of their plants in the window, touching the leaves and feeling the earth around them?) It was beginning to seem as if I had always known only this cold, a crisp, dry, skin-shrinking, lung-freezing cold.

I wondered if I could endure another day? I dreamed of sunshine, growing flowers and warm earth, but I awoke to reality and more snow. It began to haunt me. I wanted to be free of this icy grip and to see it gone. I willed it away, like King Canute ordering back the waves, but it turned around and blew in my face. I then tried ignoring it. However, in the small cottage I was unable to look out of a window or open a door, for there it was.

I searched for signs of spring, and found no indications of it arriving. No ducks or geese flew over, back to their summer home on the marsh. There wasn't a sign of robins or crows. The chickadees and snow buntings were still about, as if they had no intention of leaving to go north to their summer residence. Winter wore on, and all the while the mitts and toques gathered more holes and the snow boots and parkas were always wet from their outside journeys.

I couldn't say how I loathed it and that I'd had enough. They would have thought me feeble stuff indeed. Why didn't the others mind, I wondered? Perhaps it was the way the Manitobans used winter to their advantage, and learned to enjoy it. Snow and winter in Manitoba meant ice-hockey, watching and playing. From the age of seven, small boys talked about being on the 'Pee-Wee' team, the 'Midgets' or the 'Minors'. Winter meant a hockey uniform, shoulder pads and a jock and getting out on the ice.

Sports-minded adults took up curling, a sport with stone and broom the Scots had brought over. This game could take them through the winter happily, with bonspiel after bonspiel to keep them hurrying off with their broom tucked underneath their arm.

To many it was a time to take up a hobby, to sew, weave or tat ready for the next 'Home Bake and Sew Sale' for the missionary society. To young girls it was a time for figure skating and practising for the tests and the skating review held in April. There were few prairie children who were not experts on skates, even I found I could skate when we bought second-hand pairs for ourselves and Richard and a pair of bob-skates (with two blades) for Peter and went on the farm slew.

But I didn't curl and I had no sewing machine and I couldn't go skating very often, so there was the snow to shovel from the door again and the path to remake to the goat shed.

Then suddenly, as secretly as winter had arrived, spring bounced in, as if she had been waiting round the corner for a certain day to make an entrance. The sun was pouring through the window, a warm sun that made the icicles drip all day and the snow on the south side turn to slush. It was so warm that the boys sank down into their favourite snow hill, the one that had the flag and was Scott at the North Pole. We had to go and rescue them.

It was really spring. In fact it was hot! The snow shrunk more and more each day and I watched it with a light heart. It would soon be puddles, then I saw a host of robins pecking in the yard, as if they had been hiding round the corner waiting for their entrance!

Of course there were other cold days and it tried vainly to snow, but the sun was now in full command and cold gave way to warm. In less than two weeks the snow had disappeared, except in the shadiest corners.

We kept going outside to breathe in the mild, sweet air and the scent of earth and grass, almost forgotten. We felt drunk on it! We were being conquering heroes. We beat our chests. We had survived our first Manitoba winter. We hadn't frozen, though we certainly thought we might at times. We hadn't starved, just been hungry now and then, and as primitive as our living had been we had shrugged off winter in our cramped, fusty little lair and had come out as bushy-tailed and bright-eyed as groundhogs, and hardly a sniffle or a sore throat.

I hung out the snowsuits and parkas. I washed everything in sight. I scrubbed the cottage from top to bottom and we took down the storm windows and storm door and hid them away in the garage again. We shook the soot from the stove pipes and put them back up and I bought tomatoes and lettuce for salads. I went with the children and picked fuzzy mauve Manitoba crocus where Aggie said they grew and I set them on the table smiling. Winter was but a memory.

Annabelle added to our giddy spring feeling by having a family of two white kids, a male and female. We quickly named them Snowdrop and Billy. Less than a week later Nanny had a daughter and we called her Snowflake. The two new mothers were as happy at their kids' arrival as we were. They were also quite happy to let us rear their kids for them. Nanny had an udder too large for any tiny kid goat to tackle, so she gently pushed her towards us as an offering.

Richard and Peter soon learned to feed them from a bottle and Susy tried as well. Soon the six kids together were inseparable and a water barrel on its side was all they needed to keep them happy, with children climbing in and kids jumping on, or the other way round.

The goats sat in the sun and watched them all at play, happy to have such willing baby sitters. I rather thought, when the boys went running to the farm to play with Bob, the goat mothers could have looked after them, but then the kids ran to me and their mothers hid in the hedge, so I guessed goats and I and all mothers had a lot in common. Kids are nice but it's nicer to have someone to look after them for a while.

We decided to make further use of the sheds that were behind the cottage by renovating them a little and raising capons in them. We bought a hundred chicks, of a heavy breed. After a month we moved them off the shelf to the floor space and bought a hundred more for the shelf.

The long winter had taught us to preserve all of summer that we could, to 'gather ye rosebuds', for now we realized how short and sweet a prairie summer was. George kindly gave us a corner of the field by the cottage to start a garden, and he cultivated it for us with the rest of the land. We raked and made the soil fine and then planted every vegetable we could name, some for summer's use and the rest for winter storage and canning. We planted sunflowers for the children, a row of flowers for me, water melon and cantaloupe to see if we could grow them (and for something to write home about), and a few extra rows for Annabelle, Nanny, and their kids.

I was letting the goats off their tether for a while each day and I thought the best time was while I was in the garden busy weeding. Yet they would creep up behind me and thin some more rows I had already thinned, and if they were not there they would be in the house because I hadn't closed the door properly. That pleased Annabelle. She had no use for my bread but she loved the *Reader's Digest* and I would find her sitting on the couch enjoying them all. I couldn't keep ahead of them. If I remembered to shut the door I would forget to look behind me in the garden. I was so absorbed in the gardening. So I tethered them again and we took them for walks. Christopher shook his head at me. 'I told you they couldn't be trusted,' he said knowingly.

'Yes they can. They are curious and have to try things, that's all.' I always stood up to defend them and I reminded him of all the milk they had given us.

'They didn't give it, you took it,' he told me, showing off again.

Christopher was pleased with himself. Although garage work wasn't his aim in life he now had steady employment and that meant money in the bank waiting for our farm. It also meant trading off the van for a car. We said goodbye to her sadly all the same. She had brought us a long way. The Austin he drove home was spanking clean and just polished and he inspected our hands before we could touch. Richard sat at the wheel and made car noises and Peter and Susy bounced on the seats. 'Let's go for a ride dad!'

'Can't now. On Sunday we shall all go for a nice long drive.'

We must have been determined to make the most of summer. The past winter, our first on the prairie (we were told it had been the worst on record since 1824—we thought they were all like that!) had given us a longing, almost an obsession, to make the most of summer.

Early on Sunday morning we filled the trunk of the car with towels and sweaters and the picnic basket and were away to see more of Manitoba.

'We're coming back, aren't we?' Richard's voice was anxious. He was remembering the last time we had packed things and taken a long journey.

'Of course we are,' I assured him. 'This is our home.'

Was it our home? When does an immigrant call his new country home? Does it have to await the following generations to have that distinction and are we always immigrants? We felt it to be our home, as if it had entered our blood. We had faced its winter, everything it had threatened us with, and it hadn't daunted us. We had shared the joys and sorrows of our neighbours, and would share more. I was becoming a Canadian though I was a Londoner, a Cockney, and I made Cockney mistakes.

However, I promised Christopher I would never ask another gentleman if he got a good screw. I told him the man was talking about salaries and so was I. How was I to know that 'screw' was a colloquialism for intercourse? And I never said 'Were you diddled, love?' again. It was worrying to have someone, with a smirk on his face, take you aside and say, 'Diddle? How do you do that?'

Yet our backs were not turned on the country of our birth. We loved her more. We loved the memory of her hustle and bustle, her sense of humour, her stubbornness and her character, and we knew that all around us, on the prairie and off, were the offspring of the characters England had moulded. Yes, we did feel it was 'home'!

We drove westward, away from the flat prairie. First we went to the Pioneer Museum at Austin to see the implements and vehicles that had opened up the West. We stood on the mighty steam tractors that had pulled the breaking ploughs. We examined the Red River carts. They were made entirely of wood, and had squeaked across the prairie carrying her first settlers. We saw the cutters and democrats, horse-drawn vehicles that the next generation had gone to church and town in. We saw the covered waggon, and we imagined the cruel and bumpy ride it had given the pioneer family inside. I could feel akin to the sad-irons, the lamps and the butter churn. I could talk about them as well!

When we had seen enough of what the pioneer (the good guys) had done to claim the West, we drove to Carberry Hills and the 'bad lands' where only a brave Indian had dared to venture. We followed the hot, dry, barren desert, where the only shade was a gnarled and stunted oak and only rough bush and prickly cactus grew, ugly, dusty and deformed, derelicts of nature in the shifting grey-brown sand.

We walked up the sharp buttes that hid the view ahead and were suddenly halted by the sight of the valley below. Green growth was lush on either side of the winding Assinaboine River. There it wasn't difficult to imagine a horseman of the past rejoicing with parched throat on seeing the valley below.

We could have travelled all day around the lonely desert trails. The only living sight was a racoon at the bark of a tree, a gopher, or a skunk, large and hairy, his broad white stripe down his back saying 'beware!' When a crane arose from the scrub and on slender legs reached for the sky, we were grateful for the sight of beauty in the wilderness and the knowledge now that there must be water near.

It was hot, dry and still and this was Canada in the rough where life held tenuously. It was the edge of habitation, and in the sun-caked stillness that held us, hot, dizzy, breathing in the dry air, it was hard to remember that another world existed. How far away were the primroses now? Were there really trim lawns, and did people still play croquet before a tea of wafer-thin cucumber sandwiches and madeira cake beneath the laburnums? Were they still there?

While we were stepping on a cactus, was the vicar still riding down an English country lane, his bicycle wobbling as he nodded to Mrs Martin? With sand funnelling a whirlwind across this dry desert land, were they still changing the guard at Buckingham Palace?

We shouldn't linger. We knew how easy it was to succumb to the heat so we drove away, away from the 'badlands' where the Indians rode no longer and the cowboys had gone to greener pastures. We drove home, stopping to finish the freshie and eat the rest of the sandwiches and taking a stick to see the fish in the Assinaboine.

The sun was setting when we again reached the prairie. We had come away from the hills and out of the valley and driven past the woodlands until we were away from the trees and on the prairie proper. Vast stretches of pale, growing grain now welcomed us and over it all was a canopy of blue.

As dusk approached nothing could hide the sun in its evening ritual of retiring. Its blushing ray filled the sky. It was a glowing performance and half the world the stage while sitting in the front, getting the best view, were the prairies. The world was set to flame as the sun made her obeisance to the moon and the sky cooled to a rose pink in the afterglow. The rose deepened to crimson as the sun became languorous, then a gossamer haze veiled her boudoir, aware of her nakedness, and finally the evening dusk covered her up.

Margaret Wolfe jumped off her bicycle and stopped at the cottage. She told me that the missionary ladies were going 'Saskatoon hunting' the next day and if I would like to go too I should be at the farm after lunch. 'And Donna said leave the kids with her, she doesn't mind.'

I said, 'Yes, sure. I'll be there,' as any mother would at the chance of going away for a while.

The boys jumped for joy. 'Woweee. Bob is home on vacation. I'll take my bat for baseball, zipperdy doo!' I stared at Richard. He had an English mother and he was talking with a Canadian accent!

When I thought about it after Margaret had left, I wondered. Why would they want to hunt for Saskatoons? Didn't Saskatoons live in Saskatchewan as Manitobans live in Manitoba? Why then were they hunting for them in Manitoba? Perhaps there was some old feud arising like 'those damn Yankees', so once in a while they hunted them out. It all sounded very unusual, but if the missionary ladies were game I could be too. I didn't know what to wear for the expedition but I thought blue jeans would be wise, they were sturdy. When I reached the farm with the children, the other members were there, wearing trousers too, also heavy shirts, sun hats, or caps. It was an odd array. Aggie looked as if she meant business in George's old pants, Jim's cowboy shirt, high boots and a baseball cap.

'You can't hunt for Saskatoons in that thin blouse,' she warned me. 'You'll have it torn off or get bitten to death.'

'I will?'

'Of course. I'll get you one of Bob's long-sleeve shirts.'

'She's not wearing a belt,' someone else noticed. 'Have to get some twine around you. You need both hands for Saskatoons. It's easier to get at them.'

'It is?' I didn't want to appear a coward, but I wanted to know how big they were.

'Where are the Saskatoons?' I asked instead.

'Well, we are going into the bush across the river. That's where we usually find them.'

'You don't find them everywhere then?'

'Oh no. We are going into the bush across the river. That's where the darn things usually hang out.' Lizzie chuckled. 'Always where it's hard to get at them.'

We went in two cars. I noticed they didn't seem at all concerned, quite excited in fact, and were discussing things unmissionary, like who was having a baby and so soon after the wedding and other racy subjects.

We drove through Portgage and on over the bridge across the Assinaboine, into the sandhills and bush country. The country was thick with trees and an easy place to be lost in but the driver seemed to know where we were going, and she stopped down a narrow trail.

'A farmer down here said they were everywhere in this bush if we hunted,' Ruth said. I wondered why he couldn't hunt the Saskatoons himself instead of calling on the missionary ladies.

'We're right behind you,' Lizzie called from the other car.

Everyone jumped out eagerly. I stood back, hoping I'd be forgotten. Then someone gave me a pail.

'Tie it on to your belt.'

'What for?'

'Easier to put the Saskatoons in.'

'I put the Saskatoons in the pail?'

'Yes dear, unless you plan to eat them all.'

We went in two groups and each group said they would yell when they found them. They strode into the dense bush.

'Keep close behind me, you don't want to get lost,' Aggie warned. Her words were needless. I was on her heels. Suddenly there was a loud 'Yoo hoo over here. We've found some.'

'Come quick, they've found them.' Aggie pushed ahead through the tangle of bush to reach the other group who were busy picking things off trees. They were little purple berries and they were delicious.

I had seen Aggie and the other women busy canning. I had a recipe book and I was determined to learn. Canning was another time-honoured custom. In fact it was a necessity if they wished to eat well all winter. Fruit, vegetables and meat were preserved in glass sealers and usually stored in the basement. I was going to put them on the shelf, and once I started canning I was 'hooked'. Everything I could grow, gather from the bushes and trees, or buy when there was an over-abundance and it was sold cheaply, I bought and put into sealers.

It started with rhubarb. I used it with onions and herbs first to make a sweet relish. Rhubarb with oranges made an interesting marmalade, and rhubarb, versatile as it was, blended with other fruits, taking their flavour and making them go further.

As the vegetables ripened I canned what I did not need for the table. I was given sealers by people who had deep freezers, the modern way to preserve, and so didn't use them any more. I used them all. I couldn't bear to see a sealer empty. I had to fill it.

I was determined that we wouldn't go hungry the next winter, and to see the cupboard shelves filling up with preserves gave me a good feeling of security. It was like having my own grocery shop, and I enjoyed the colours—green relish, orange marmalade, raspberries red and strawberries redder. Saskatoons were purple and the rest of the fruit and vegetables to come. I even had something yellow when there was a sale of grapefruit.

Summer had lengthened into a reliable sameness. Warm, a little breezy, or just plain hot. Then it was difficult to arouse one's lethargy and do anything but sit and drink freshie with the kids. But I wasn't complaining. I had only to remember the last winter to rush outside and appreciate the sun. I gauged the summer by the wheat. So high, heads beginning to form, still pale green but turning a little yellow at the edges. Very good, still quite a lot of summer to go.

We had taken a few trips to Lake Manitoba, so, on a hot sultry Sunday in August, the thought of cool water and a swim made us hurry to throw towels and lunch in the Austin and head for Delta.

Manitoba was the Province of 100,000 lakes, so water was never far distant. Delta, where the lake crept safely over sand bars, was fifteen miles away. It was a sheltered cove for swimming and boating and fishing. It was a home for the thousands of wild ducks that nested there in the reeds and marshes.

We didn't care for the look of the sky that Sunday. In the north-west it was black and blue, looking like an enormous bruise, but we were sweltering, and we hoped whatever it was doing in the sky it would go the other way and do it. We were going for a swim. The temperature was ninety in the shade.

'Mad dogs and Englishmen,' I sang as we raced to the car.

'Hurry daddy, hurry!' Peter was ahead.

'Last one in is a monkey's uncle,' Richard yelled.

'That's me, that's me!' Susy ran on fat legs.

'The sky looks strange,' Christopher muttered.

But we were in high spirits and we didn't care about the purple sky in the north. It was hot and we wondered why we didn't meet other cars rushing to and from the beach as we usually did. We travelled the winding road kicking up dust and already we smelled the marsh beds, where ducks, yellow legs and sandpipers as well as many other shore birds nested. Today they were hidden.

Closer to the lake the sky became more forbidding and the air was pregnant with silence, as if listening.

'I think we are in for a bit of a storm,' Christopher said (which happened to be one of his British understatements).

Then the car swayed, hit by a sudden gust of wind, and the reeds of the marsh were swaying. We turned the bend that led us on to the beach.

'What's that?' We all stared ahead. It appeared to be a giant smoky black ball and it was racing towards us. Christopher stopped, and we stared in horror.

'Good heavens! It's a tornado ... It's coming for us!' His voice was shrill, and swinging into action he backed the car and swung round to run away. We were a small grey rabbit to the hairy grey hound that followed.

The wind had grown in strength and buffeted the little Austin from side to side. I kept looking behind to see how close the black ball was coming and the children huddled in the back seat not sure whether to laugh or cry at this strange experience.

'It's getting closer, drive faster,' I whispered.

'It won't go any faster.' He looked round. 'Shall I turn in that lane by the trees?'

'No, no, don't stop. The trees are beginning to snap. We're too close. Keep going.' We fled by the tormented trees which were making salaams to the forceful wind.

'It's getting dark, mommy,' Richard said quietly from the back seat.

''Cos that damn thing is gaining on us,' Christopher muttered.

'Because there's a thunder cloud, dear,' I said louder.

We had always noticed the stone-built church on the left of us by the road. It stood alone, a stalwart sight and with the endless prairie around I wondered who attended it. Now its deep front porch stood out as welcoming arms. Christopher pulled into the churchyard and we all rushed in and through the blessedly open doors while the black ball, tapering funnel-wise to a tail, rushed by us straight on its course. It was followed by torrential rain, but the danger was gone. We drove home with the windshield wipers splashing and the wheels sending up sprays of water.

We heard later that the 'twister', as they were commonly called, had lifted the roofs from grain bins, and upturned sheds and chicken houses that were in its path. It had buckled barns and made pretzels of television aerials. No one had been injured, though it had left a trail of damage that made us wonder why we had not stayed at home like sensible Canadians, instead of going out to play tag with a 'twister'.

We were now aware that Manitoba summers were hot and of short duration, and you might as well enjoy every moment of that sunshine for 'It's a long, long winter!'

But the days raced by. June was the song 'Bustin' out all over', for with warm encouraging showers of rain the growth of everything was phenomenal. Then came blousy July when we wished it was cooler and that the fruits and vegetables wouldn't all ripen at once (busy canning, I couldn't keep up with it). August was pleasant and the nights cool, and 'fall' arrived all too soon.

On the prairie, school commenced earlier than in the cities and towns, allowing for lost days when the children were 'storm-stayed'. Opening day was July 28th, and Richard eligible enough for grade one.

I bought him a pair of new pants. 'Big boy kind,' he insisted, 'not the ones with elastic in the back!' He had a white shirt too for the first day. He left on foot for the little red school house carrying his lunch pail and a clean handkerchief. (When I told Aggie I was buying a lunch pail she said, 'Wait until I've looked in Grandma's room,' and she searched and came out, dusty but triumphant, with a serviceable one.)

He walked down the road between the stubble, small and brave. I watched him getting smaller and smaller into the distance, trying to control the lump in my throat. At the farm gate, he went in the car with the Wolfe children who also attended the one-room school with grades from one to eight.

He wasn't as brave the next morning or as eager. He

refused to walk on and stubbornly kicked at the gravel on the road outside the cottage. I shooed him away, telling him to go, knowing I was really 'driving him from the nest'. Then a few days later, the teacher, wise to her class ranging from 'babies' to 'stalwart farm boys wearing boots', took him aside and asked him if he would tidy her desk, seeing as he was in the front row. He suddenly felt special and important then, and he also fell promptly in love with her, for he talked of her constantly. So I waved him away and he waved back gaily and raced down the road as I controlled another lump in my throat, and wondered if I would mind so much when the other children started school.

We were anticipating winter this time and we were well prepared. The citron was ripe and I made a different marmalade that no one liked, so I cut the rest into squares and made a strange preserve, which the recipe said was 'unusual'. (It was.)

I was carried away by it all. When the watermelon ripened I went about rescuing rinds to pickle. I also pickled cucumbers and small white onions for they were too ripe. Christopher was afraid to eat anything from the garden, he said, in case it was meant to be in a jar! The tomatoes were then ready so they were canned whole, and made into soup or chili sauce, and those that didn't ripen before the frost were allowed to be green tomato chutney or left to ripen under the bed.

'Do you think I could have a fresh tomato?' Richard asked so sweetly that I left a full bowl around and watched them being eaten. I reckoned they would have filled six more sealers.

I now had only the crab-apples to 'put up', as all the other women called preserving. They were plentiful at the farm and I was let loose to pick a box full. I made apple sauce and crab-apple jelly. It must have been beginner's luck but it was my swan-song to preserving. The clear orange jelly gleamed in the jars. It looked as if the sun had crept in and I had caught it alive. I didn't think I could even let them eat that!

In September we dug up the potatoes, carrots and turnips and stored them in the goat house. We filled the garage with logs for winter, easier to fetch when the snow was deep. We dragged out the storm windows again and latched on the storm door. We next castrated the male goat in readiness for winter meat. We weren't keen, he had been our favourite one of the kids. The capons were ready to sell, except for those we kept for our own winter use.

But this year when we were all ready, winter was in no hurry at all. The storm windows were in place. The house was banked with earth. I had a sack of flour in the bin and extra groceries in the cupboard, so that we were all prepared if we should suddenly be snowed in, but nothing happened. We were beginning to feel rather ridiculous. Our shelter was ready. The house was barricaded, our ammunition was hidden, and nothing attacked us. There weren't even hostile Indians any more!

Grandma Wolfe died. She was old and tired and the leaves were falling. It was time to go. She lay in the big bed and turned her face to the wall, begging them with tired eyes to be patient with her and let her go peacefully.

There was no need for a doctor. Prairie folk looked after their own. Carrie, who always sat with the dying, came at once and other relations and neighbours took a spell so that Grandma was never alone as she waited.

She lay in the bed, a tiny, frail figure, while familiar sounds went on about her—the cry of children, the rattling of plates, and the sound of the men's heavy boots being removed in the porch.

Grandma was respected. She had come from Ireland as a young woman, from a fine home with servants, but following the man she loved. But if the first home had been made of logs she still retained her genteel and refined manner. The log shack floor was earth packed hard (hard enough to polish, they say) but she put Irish linen on the table and on the bed. Visitors ate from fine china and remembered their manners in front of Grandma Wolfe. Butter wasn't a slab. Her home-made butter was patted into curls. The winter might be harsh and a man had to be tough, but in Grandma's eyes he still behaved like a gentleman. The summers made them sweat like pigs, and behind the barn they might say so, but in Grandma's house they 'perspired'.

When she went to church, and it was every Sunday winter and summer except when the church was closed for harvest, her horse was groomed and the brass accoutrements on the democrat were rubbed to shine. But then Grandma Wolfe was typical of many pioneers, who not only brought their determination and muscle to their new country but morals, good manners and decency as well.

Now as she lay in the big bed, brought over from Ireland, with family and friends around her, she lay at peace and with a gentle sigh, she passed away.

I stayed at the farm on the day of the funeral to help prepare the lunch. The best table was set with Irish linen and the best china. The crusts were removed from the sandwiches (and fed to the hens, of course). The glass cloth was out ready and there were fine linen napkins instead of paper serviettes. The example Grandma had always set had not been in vain. She would have approved.

Friends and relations came back from the graveyard and sat down in their Sunday best, secretly tugging at collars and ties and pushing back thoughts that it being such a fine day they ought to be working on the land. They made a solemn gathering and were not their usual good-humoured selves until Bob came in with the gopher and it jumped out of his hands. Darting under a chair the gopher resembled a rat. In fact the women thought it was a rat and we raced each other to the chairs. The men crawled in pursuit of the furry brown animal, each trying to be the one to catch it.

It turned out not such a sad funeral after all. In fact it was rather fun.

'Mother wouldn't have minded,' George smiled. 'Buays will be buays,' she often said, and I noticed then how Irish George could sound, though a long way and a long time from Skibereen. 'No, Grandma didn't like people sitting around doleful. She liked a bit of fun,' he told us. I think Grandma knew that was a necessary attribute for the people of the prairie, too.

If the weather was holding back the missionary ladies were on the war path. It was just when we were beginning to feel we belonged on the prairie. I was even beginning to sound Canadian, I thought. Well, I had never said, 'How yer makin' out?' back in England and I was careful not to say anything to offend any more, though to me they had been innocent remarks. As what I am about to tell must have been. I was in the village store buying some groceries. The owner and I were talking about the price of food, milk, and the raising of children.

'I guess the kids drink plenty of milk,' she said.

'Not any more,' I told her. 'They drink water now.' I reached for the marmalade on the shelf.

'They do?' She looked surprised. 'Don't they like milk?'

'Oh yes. They would drink it all if we let them, but we want it ourselves.' At the time I noticed she looked puzzled and stared at me, but I didn't think it important and forgot about it. Then people started asking how the kids were. 'I never see them outside now,' another said.

'No. I don't let them out. I keep them in all the time now.'

'Yes, but don't they get restless and want to be outside?'

'I guess so, always at the door, but it's such a bother getting them in again.'

'But my dear, the fresh air is good for them.'

'I know,' I agreed, 'but they are so bad when they are out, climbing on things, running away, and I have to chase down the road after them. They enjoy it, I know, but it is less work keeping them in.'

Donna would sometimes walk down to the cottage in the evening and she was company when Christopher worked in the evenings and the children were sleeping. She was glancing towards the bedroom when she spoke.

'My, those kids are cute,' she sighed. 'I wouldn't mind having one myself.'

'You would? I guess they are rather pets at times but they are also a darn nuisance. One was trying to eat the labels off the cans, they will nibble at everything.'

'Are they hungry, do you think?' Donna asked worriedly.

'No. I don't think so, just bad kids. I could shoot them some days.'

'Oh please don't say that. What if you lost them? Give them to me. I will look after them. I love kids.'

'Very well,' I laughed. 'If we have any more I will give it to you. I told Christopher we haven't room for more so if we do he'll have to kill it at birth. It's the kindest way.'

Donna gasped. 'You wouldn't do that, would you?' She pushed her chair away and left soon after.

I think it was about then that I thought the missionary ladies were acting rather strangely. I wasn't invited to the following meeting, maybe they forgot to tell me, but they didn't usually forget.

They still liked the children. Richard was invited in for glasses of milk on the way home from school and one evening the children were all taken in for supper. I wasn't asked.

The climax came at the next meeting. I asked them not to forget me. I was supposed to help with the programme. They said 'Hello' and 'How are you?' when I arrived, but I felt they were avoiding me and giving me sidelong glances when I wasn't looking, or did I imagine it?

Later, when the meeting was over and tea was served, the minister's wife, who was friendly to all, came and sat by me.

'I saw the kids playing outside the other day, my they are so cute. If I hadn't had to hurry I would have stopped to play with them and visit you.'

'Oh yes, they are rather cute, sometimes, but they are getting bigger and really not so cute as they were. It must have been the day they got out and I had to chase them in, they hadn't been out for ages so were terrors to catch.'

'Don't you let them out to get the fresh air?' She was looking surprised and I noticed there was silence. Everyone was listening. 'Well it must be a chore, with such active little ones, and dressing them warmly,' she added kindly.

'Oh I don't dress them,' I told her, wondering what she

thought I put on them.

'But don't they get cold?' she asked in a shocked voice.

'No, they don't feel the cold, they are pretty tough you know and the house isn't warm, so they are used to the cold.'

'It isn't warm?' she said in a worried voice. (Maybe she belongs to the humane society, I thought.) She then put her hand on my arm to prepare me for a personal question. 'Have you plenty of blankets for them dear?'

'Blankets?' I laughed out loud despite her anxious look. 'Kids don't need blankets, they have straw.'

'Straw?'

'Yes, they have plenty of fresh straw to lie on. It's all they need,' I assured her.

Solemnly now she asked and I felt the whole room was waiting for my answer.

'You have three kids, haven't you?'

'No only two now. We decided to eat one. Though,' I confided, 'we won't enjoy him. When you bottle-raise them you do get so attached to them.'

The minister's wife gasped and looked as if she would faint. It was Aggie who explained, between sips of hot tea hastily given to the minister's wife, that I was talking about goat kids (she hoped I was, no doubt), while she, the minister's wife, was talking about children.

To me kids were young goats and children were children. It was just a misinterpretation and I hoped it cleared things up.

And I thought I was so Canadian. I said 'Hi' to everyone instead of hello. I asked Christopher to 'fix it' instead of mend, and I said 'holy cow' as if I had always spoken that way. I nearly always said 'the fall' instead of autumn, and 'candy' not sweets.

I drank coffee and sometimes coke. We ate corn on the cob and things like bacon and pancakes with syrup. We never forgot which side of the road to drive on and we had learned to eat with the fork in our right hand (even though we felt like our own nanny, doing so). I had almost forgotten what a 'bob' was and I never said 'fortnight'. Instead of saying 'Cor stone the crows', it was 'Gosh and gee whizz'. 'Balony' took the place of 'codswallop'. I sometimes told the children 'not to be sassy kids' instead of 'shut up you little b——s'.

Yes, I still used English expressions and I still made mistakes, and the latest was almost as silencing as the one before when I informed the missionary ladies that 'Christopher was getting home at three-thirty after having worked a night shift and I told him to knock me up as soon as he got in as I wanted to put the bread on to rise.'

I never knew why I sat alone at that meeting either!

TEN

A WINTER OF ILLNESS

Several snowfalls had now settled us down for winter so we felt our preparation had been wise after all. To be truthful, we were feeling rather proud of ourselves.

'Hydro' was installed. White electric light bulbs showed up the corners and shabby spots and the cottage lost its tender glow. We bought a refrigerator and a hot-plate, an electric iron and a toaster, so we felt really modernized, but we stayed loyal to the wood stove. There was a subtle defiance putting another log on the fire while looking out in the eye of a snowstorm. Electricity could fail us but while we had wood, which we had hewn ourselves, we weren't intimidated, and the pioneer woman wasn't disappointed in me. In addition we had all our preserves, our meat and laying hens and milking goats.

With such affluence, plus money we had saved, we talked boldly about buying a farm. We decided we would start looking for a place in the spring. With the long winter ahead it would be something to plan and look forward to. We didn't know that just around the corner of our life were further setbacks, more trials to test us.

As most young couples do when they marry, we had wanted a family. The more the merrier, we cooed. This, of course, was before we knew the facts of life, such as that children cost money to bring into the world. They need lots of clothes, bedrooms, and they eat a lot too. So now when I found there was another baby on the way we were joyful, but the joy was tinged with worry.

'Where will we put another baby?' I asked, looking round the three tiny rooms.

'The Indians sling them in hammocks from the ceiling,' Christopher said, looking around the ceiling. I didn't smile so he added quickly, 'Don't worry, we will have a larger house next spring.'

The first setback came just when he thought how well he was progressing. Agriculture was at a standstill in winter on the prairie and there was a lot of unemployment, so he felt himself fortunate to be in a related field at the garage and dealing with farm machinery. Then suddenly his position was given to another man, a relation of the employer. Perhaps angry, hurt at having been treated so casually, he skidded at an icy corner and buckled the front of the car into a hydro pole.

However, we took this blow stoically enough. The problems weren't insurmountable any more. He would find other employment, and if the car was damaged, he was unhurt. We enjoyed his company and I liked having the water and wood carried in for me. We had a radio. It was a novelty, more proof of man's tenacity. However bleak the scene, we could listen entranced to the music, a radio play, full of trustful belief that the hero would conquer the foe. We would blink an eye at the sad parts and were never bored or blasé.

Christopher made me learn chess for there was no one else to play against, but Dicky watched carefully and was soon to tell me I had made a wrong move and he became a better opponent than I and took over. We were close, tight-knit, sufficient unto ourselves. The prairie in winter decreed that we be, and we were optimistic. We had lived through one Manitoba winter so we could face anything. When the children were abed we planned our farm and Christopher was looking for another job and we all looked to the future hopefully.

The children had sailed through the measles and chicken-pox when it went around the district so when they awoke with sore throats and swollen glands we wondered if they had the mumps. I was going to ask Aggie the next morning but Peter was so sore and sick we bundled them up and took them to the doctor. It was swollen glands and we took home the medicine and applied the hot fomentations. Susy was fine but wore a scarf in sympathy and Dicky wanted to go back to school, only Peter remained listless. The swelling didn't subside. He fought against the hot fomentations and only wanted to be left alone, straight and still in his bed. Fighting his high temperature, we took turns bathing him through the night and went back to the doctor the next morning.

We waited while the doctor examined him and he soon reappeared, his face serious. 'Take him at once to hospital. He has meningitis!'

At the Portage hospital, a cottage hospital, the nurses took command and carried him away and asked us to leave and await the outcome of the tests. Words of warning drummed in my head. 'It is cruel to take such small children to a strange country and expect them to endure what you might have to face.'

Fools rush in! Fingers pointed at me accusingly. 'Christopher, you should think of the children. What if one of them is sick or you are? How are you going to pay the bills? Things are different over there.' They had thrown up their hands in dismay at our leaving security, our families and home, to sail away to Canada on nothing but a pipe dream. Yet with the courage of our abilities we had ignored them and gone ahead. 'Stop being so pessimistic,' we had turned and told them. 'Look at us. We're young and healthy so nothing like that will happen.' (To others perhaps, but not to us.) Was it now we paid the price? All their fears and warnings culminating in this one final blow? If so, they were right. We had lost.

You don't have to ask for help on the prairies. Emily stayed with the children when we walked to the farm early the next morning. Christopher called the hospital, and turned to me. 'Peter is worse. They want us to take him to the Children's Hospital in Winnipeg right away.'

There was no ambulance service available in Portage at the time, so George at once said we should take the Chrysler. 'It will take you there faster,' he told us, and hurried away to fill the gas tank while Aggie went for warm blankets.

A nurse was waiting with Peter and she carried him to the car, holding him watchfully at the back, asking me to sit in the front. I looked at the small, lifeless stranger she held and heard the rattle in his throat and the shallow movement of his chest as he laboured for breath.

We went as fast as safety would allow along the narrow winding highway, past miles of open prairie and lonely churches, feeling a small swell of hope that people could come from afar to gather at these emblems of faith standing stark but assured on the windswept prairie. I stared, and could only hear the struggle for breath and the nurse taking anxious looks at Peter and diverting my attention to other things.

We reached the village of St Francis Xavier but there was still another thirty miles ahead. Christopher pushed the car faster and then a tyre blew and the heavy car was swerved to a stop.

'There's a spare. Won't take long,' Christopher reassured us and jumped out.

The car lay at an obtuse angle to the ditch and he couldn't raise the car with the jack. I stood helplessly by. The nurse was looking back for help. She said we must stop the first car that came along, but the road was bare, we were alone. I noticed a farm down the lane to our right and without another word I raced to it.

An elderly woman answered my frantic knocking on the door and seeing my distraught face she quickly called her husband. They spoke little English and I repeated my request with desperate pantomime. The woman spoke quickly to her husband in German and he took me to his car parked in a garage.

He drove carefully to the highway where the nurse was out of the Chrysler ready with Peter. She climbed in and we drove away, leaving Christopher to struggle with the tyre.

The Mennonite farmer, I was sure, had never driven his car at a great speed but he had seen the child and the nurse and he perhaps then drove the fastest he had ever driven before.

'As soon as we reach the city outskirts I want to stop a patrol car. The hospital is the other side so I want a police escort through the traffic.' The nurse spoke with professional authority and I nodded, scanning the traffic as soon as we approached the city. She told the farmer to wave down the first police car that approached. Without speaking, seeing the nurse and child, the police officer turned his car round and helped us in, setting his lights flashing and siren blasting before speaking. 'I can get you there faster this way. Children's?' The nurse nodded yes, and thanked him.

I didn't speak. I hadn't thanked the farmer who had brought us this far. I was watching the nurse, who had covered Peter's face. He was now very still and the raspings had ceased, but I hadn't the courage to ask her....

With sirens blaring, keeping the road clear, the patrol car raced to the hospital. When I looked back I saw Christopher driving the Chrysler close behind. I told the police officer what had happened.

'He's been close for a while. I guessed he was the child's father, I saw his face,' he murmured with understanding.

When the car stopped in front of the hospital I expected the nurse to walk slowly with her burden, but as the car stopped she had the door open and she fled with him around the corner to 'Emergency', leaving us to follow.

We waited. We sat and watched busy nurses wheeling sick children along corridors. Doctors walked by with faces full of concern, and parents like ourselves were anxiously waiting, lost in their own world of worry. Later a doctor beckoned us to a small office and he waited until we were seated before he spoke. 'Peter is very ill. We are taking more tests and beginning treatment.' He put a long form in front of us that we had to fill in. He took it and looked up. 'We will do all we can. There is no point in your seeing him. He is in a private room and he won't know you anyway. I want you to go home.' He looked knowingly at my bulging coat. 'You have other children to think of and it will do you no good waiting.' I looked away.

'Go home,' he said more gently. 'We will phone you if there is any change.'

We walked away slowly. The nurse was waiting at the entrance. She had removed her surgical mask and we saw her face, not just the eyes, which gave too much away with the mouth not there to defend them.

It was a strange journey home. Maybe in times of great stress or grief one enters a void of nothingness, and floating in this abyss you aren't aware that life is going on around you, or perhaps it is shock and the brain is numb. This is nature's way (or is it God's?) of lifting the load that is too much to bear.

We turned again into the lane to the farmhouse, the lane I ran down so desperately only a few hours (or was it a lifetime) ago. We stood at the door and thanked the farmer and his wife. The wife put her hands together in prayer. 'Your son will be in our prayers.' She spoke in halting English but there were tears in her eyes and we walked away, the lane a blur.

We didn't hurry home, there seemed nothing to hurry to. I wanted to be with Peter. I felt I had deserted him, but I knew I must think of the other children, the baby that stirred inside me. We knew the possibility of Peter recovering was just a thread of hope. Our savings for the farm would pay the hospital and doctor's fees and we would somehow have to carry on.

Before we reached Portage we stopped at a restaurant. I realized then that we hadn't eaten that day and for some unknown reason I wanted an ice-cream. I didn't even care for ice-cream that much. Maybe it was the thought that ice-cream was for children and a corner of the mind remembered what it was to be happy and without care. I thought it odd to be eating ice-cream just the same and wondered vaguely what would be the proper thing to eat?

Peter's condition remained unchanged the next day. We had phoned again early. Christopher took my arm. 'We can only go home and wait until there is better news,' he told me firmly. 'There's nothing we can do to hasten it. He is in their hands, and God's. Be patient.' He knew I felt lost and far away from such a little boy. He helped me over the snowdrifts and we trudged our way home. Early the next morning we were startled by a loud rap at the door and Aggie calling us.

'It's the hospital,' her voice faltered. 'They want you to go right away.'

She helped me dress, and Emily was there dressing the other two children and she took them home with her so we could go quickly. Christopher had the car started and we drove away over snowy roads made slick with travel.

The journey was a blur of apprehension. I did have a remote hope that the car would crash, travelling as fast as we were, then we wouldn't have to face things any more, but a corner of hope quickly took over, stopping the thought.

We gave our names again at the desk and we were told to go up to 'Isolation'. There we hurried down another corridor, not knowing what we were hurrying to. Hurrying to hear dreaded words or hurrying in hope there had been a change in his condition? A doctor was walking towards us and my immediate thought was that I would be stoic and not cry out or faint and make a nuisance of myself and work for busy nurses.

'Good news,' he said at once, smiling at us. 'A few hours ago we gave his chances as almost nil, which was the reason we called you, but there has been a small improvement.' He emphasized this in fear our hopes had jumped too high. 'His temperature is down somewhat so the crisis may be over. You have to put these gowns on, then you can see him.'

He looked small and frail in the white hospital bed. Tubes protruded in various places and he looked so fragile I was afraid to touch him, so we sat by the crib and watched him breathe. As I watched each shallow breath I discovered how helpless and how deep the love a sick child presents. Not only the helplessness against the sickness that is taking its toll but the losing of a little more hope for the future, the unknown quality that might have made the world a better place to live in were they given the chance to live.

We watched him a while longer, looking for a stirring, more signs of life, but his sleep was deep. He had been on a long journey to places we knew nothing about, and we weren't yet sure if he would return.

It became a long winter of waiting. We existed. All ambition fled. It was enough getting through each day and wondering what the next phone call would bring and thinking that each day that there was no change for the worse was a step forward towards his chance of recovery.

There were the stirrings of a new baby that wasn't much thought about or even wanted then. We had to get through the winter somehow, hoping each day that things would improve. Christopher was without employment but we would face each problem one at a time, each taken in turn, for if we saw them all as a whole they were too much.

We could not visit Peter for a while and when we did the nurse told us that the doctor wished first to see us and we were taken to his office and asked to sit down again. The doctor found it difficult to tell us what we could expect and the damage the illness had left. 'He may not know you, he can't feed himself and one eye does not focus, but that will be righted in time,' he added quickly. 'It is really too soon to know what damage has been done to the brain, that remains to be seen.' He looked at his desk and waited, giving us time to understand what he was trying to tell us. 'Just accept him and love him as he is, will you?'

Once more we walked fearfully to his crib. Had we prayed too hard, been too selfish to part with him? Had part of him stayed behind on that long journey and we were now left with the consequences, to face a child without a mind?

I held out the red truck we had bought him, trying to smile, praying he would not look back with vacant stare, without knowing us. He took the toy and examined it, then slowly pulled himself up on painfully thin legs. I picked him up and held him close and he put his arms around my neck. 'Mummy,' he said, 'is daddy taking us home now?'

Peter was going to get well, we felt sure now. It was as if the weight of a dark cloud had lifted and we could see the light once more. We laughed and held him each in turn, feeling his silky hair and the softness of his cheek as if we couldn't be sure he was ours. The nurse came and we left him playing with the red truck, distracted by the gentle nurse as we went away and left him again.

We drove home like ordinary people, looking at the shop windows and noticing the bright lights and what people wore. It was good to be aware of things again.

The winter was not as harsh as our first Manitoba winter and being well prepared we were able to endure it like true Manitobians, ignoring it the best you could and pretending it wasn't so cold.

Slowly our life was shifting to an even keel again. Christopher was employed by another agricultural implement firm and garage. I made baby clothes, trying to be eager, but my thoughts were so often with a little boy sixty miles away I put the clothes aside and helped the children fill scrapbooks with bright coloured pictures to take to Peter. This way we felt closer to him, for after several more visits we stayed away because they were too upsetting for him and a setback to his getting well.

Not only was the winter docile for the best part, the days hurried by and spring and large puddles were in the yard before we were aware the snow was melting. It was the year the spring, like an anxious bride, rushed the river. The Assinaboine, a ribbon of ice, was stirred too soon and in its haste to reach the lake it went wild and huge ice-cubes jammed the river banks and spilled over. The 'Red' couldn't cope. She too was pushing eagerly westward and people spoke excitedly of flooding and harked back to the big flood of 1950. Selfishly we found ourselves unconcerned. Just when we pined to be a family all together again and wondered when it would ever be, the hospital said that

Peter was ready to go home. It was late March and he had been away six months.

I had his best clothes packed days before we could leave. They had phoned on the Wednesday and we couldn't go until Saturday. Another life-time. The car was cleaned and polished (Dicky wanted to put up the Christmas decorations again) and when Saturday came we got into our best clothes and drove to Winnipeg to bring Peter home.

His clothes were far too big for him and Susy and Dicky were as shy as strangers as Christopher carried him out to the car. They walked behind silently, not sure who the little boy was we were taking home.

After a few miles the strangeness had become familiarity and they knew that under the hospital pallor and loose clothes it was really Peter. He had a patch over his good eye, put there to strengthen the weak eye, and when I looked round Susy was wearing it. The patch soon became a problem. They all wanted one so Christopher suggested that they each have one so that Peter would keep his on. It was a good idea, though it caused strange stares when they all went around wearing them together and Dicky blackened them and they pretended they were pirates.

In May we had the same plot of land for our garden but the enthusiasm wasn't there. I also gave the living-room a fresh coat of paint but it was no good, we knew we needed a larger house. The cottage had been a haven in a time of need but we had grown out of its tiny rooms. Tentatively we looked in the paper hoping there might be something. We didn't mention a farm. We were afraid to tempt the gods. Our aspirations might be heard!

One evening, a week later, Christopher read from the newspaper, 'Forty acres here with house and barn. I wonder where it is?' He spoke as if it wasn't important one way or the other.

'Oh,' I said. I tried to sound as bored. 'I wonder?'

'Phone number here. I guess I could give them a ring some time to see where it is.'

He was home early the next evening. 'Hurry up, he said.

'We're going to see forty acres with house and barn.'

I took the potatoes off the stove and opened a can of beans and put bread in the toaster. We hurried away, not even bothering with the dishes.

'How far is it?'

'About twenty miles from here, across the river.' He dug in his pocket for a scrap of paper. 'Directions on there. Don't lose it.'

We drove through Portage, crossed the steel bridge and turned off on to a gravel road. We followed it until we were wandering down a narrow trail, a leafy lane (like an English lane, I thought). There was an opening in the trail and he pulled in and drove up to a yard and stopped the car by an empty house.

'Well, this is it,' he was smiling.

We got out slowly and looked at the house, a two-storey house leaning tiredly to one side. We put our heads crooked to see it better. Trees were around it, bushes and wild plum and high bush cranberry. Scattered everywhere were old car tyres, beer bottles and rusty tin cans.

'Want to see my friend?' Susy had edged up to us, her hand a tight fist that she was peeking through. She opened her hand.

'It's a grasshopper!' I screamed. It was a large grasshopper. We looked down in horror as they jumped all around us.

A dog had been sitting by the house. She was brown, fat and nondescript and she was walking sedately over to greet us. She wagged her tail, then sat down in front of Christopher and lifted a paw. He shook it and we all 'shook hands', and then she led us inside the house, up the broken step and through the creaking door. The house had large rooms, all needing paint and apparently devoid of cupboards. Looking around, the only refinement we could see was a yard light. (The house did have electricity.)

We followed the dog then to view the barn. Clumps of bright green clover grew where cattle had once stomped and a cow path meandered leisurely from the bush somewhere up to the barn. It was a log barn with a straw roof and inside the walls had been insulated with cow manure. The earth floor was as hard and smooth as cement and mushrooms and moss sprouted from the roof and birds had nests in the straw and fluttered about crossly at our intrusion. The barn was dark and smelled like a cave, simple as the earth it stood on.

We blinked as we left it for the sun's rays, sinking now to eye level. We looked around at the 'farm'. It was a derelict place. The earth had claimed back her own and man hadn't intervened. Seedlings had grown to saplings and encroached on every open space and now flourished.

'Terrible, isn't it?' Christopher said quietly, but I could see the dream there, returning, waiting to be fulfilled.

'Dreadful,' I agreed. We could do something with it, I thought to myself.

'Look at the grasshoppers. Place should be sprayed. Too late this year. All this bush should be cut back.'

'Look at all the junk.' I pointed to the cans and tyres fastidiously. 'Why wasn't it removed, or buried or something?' I stared at a plum tree, woody and wild but blossoming out in a white bouquet.

'No fences, and where was the garden?'

'Did you notice there was only one small cupboard in the house?'

'No one has stayed here long. Whoever built the barn put the most into it, I guess. Did you see the steps? One is broken.'

'Yes, I nearly broke a leg, and the walls inside could all do with fresh paint. That would help.'

'Saw a cracked window too, did you?'

'Yes. One at the side there. Terrible!'

'I know. Dreadful,' he agreed. The look was still in his eyes.

The birds scattered among the bushes and a scrap of bright orange flew to a tall poplar. Dicky and Peter were climbing a tree and Susy was catching another grasshopper, helped by the friendly dog.

I looked at the house and yard and saw a garden. Christopher was looking at the land with a knowing that it could be improved with care and knowledge. I saw all there was to be done and felt the pioneer woman smile knowingly. She knew what it was all about!

'We can have the place for a small down-payment and so much a month,' he ventured slowly, trying to keep the excitement from his voice. 'Oh, but it's horrible. You wouldn't want to live here.'

'Well,' I said carefully, afraid I might be heard. 'If the place was cleaned up and the inside painted and we had some cupboards...'

'I could soon put in cupboards, a sink too,' he said quickly.

'Wouldn't the goats love this bush. They'd help clear it.'

'Of course we won't have any money at first, but I'll be working. We could start with a few calves.'

'And rear them on goat's milk.'

'Later we might get a loan.'

'And build a decent house.'

'And barn.'

'There should be plenty of wild fruit for canning.'

'There is water.' He hurried to the pump in the yard and pumped out water cold and clear. We all cupped our hands and drank some.

We went back to the car and got in slowly, turning to look once more. The children had piled in, followed by the friendly dog. She sat between them, putting a paw on Susy's knee to restrain her, like a stout, patient nanny. We drove away. We were going to see the owner. We were going to buy a farm.

We could move in when we wanted. It was ours. We had signed on the dotted line and had become the owners of forty acres of land (if we could make the payments). We had found a lot of hard work and a whole new set of problems and, foolish romantics that we were, we couldn't believe our luck!

Perhaps it was the tree-lined leafy country lane or the plum tree heavy with blossom. Maybe it was the friendly dog adopting us, or the oriole gently wooing from the tree-tops. We didn't see the grasshoppers, the tangled bush, or the lop-sided house. It was a warm, sunny evening and the bush smelled of damp leaves and saskatoon blossom after rain.

We opened the windows to air the house. Christopher had put in the cupboards and we had painted the rooms. I watered the window box filled with petunias he had put where the grasshoppers couldn't reach. I smiled approval.

'Come on, old girl,' he said, helping me down the steps. 'Moving day tomorrow and a life-time of work ahead.'

ELEVEN

THE FARM

The farm, why did I call it a farm? It was a lot of trees with two open patches that we dared call fields. The trees were fast-growing poplars, some oak, with nothing mighty about them, and a few ash. Scattered among these were the wild plum, berry bushes and undergrowth that was creeping to the house. It was a jungle!

The house was built of logs, squared off and covered with rough shingle, and adjoining the house was the living-room. This must have been added later for it was built of shop-bought lumber. The barn and granary were built of pole, trees straight from the bush. The straw roof of the barn had rotted in places and fallen through the rafters, and the granary had painstakingly been lined with printer's plates. It was lop-sided, ramshackle and all uncared for but, as I went out in the early morning to call in the goats, I looked around in wonder.

Dew glistened like pearls and the heady scent of berry blossom tickled my nose. Cheeky sparrows squabbled over the straw on the barn roof and a shy warbler flew behind a leaf, not sure if she should stay. A squirrel scurried down a tree, looked me straight in the eye and was determined to. I went into the bush hoping to see the white-tailed doe with the twin fawns again, or the bushy-tailed coyote. It was Disneyland, a wonderland, and I was Alice.

Like Christopher, I saw a red barn and white-painted dairy, green meadows neatly fenced and golden cows grazing. I too saw the woods cleared of the undergrowth, giving space and shade for our Jersey herd and, where the bush was sparse, completely cleared and reseeded.

I saw a warm house with running water and an oil furnace, a flower garden around the house (I'd make them grow somehow). I would have a kitchen garden, fruit trees, garden chairs. I shook my head, it was the impossible dream. Where would we get all the money to do these marvellous things?

As I milked the goats I studied the barn. The builder must have searched diligently for the straightest, roundest trees. The circumference was the same at both ends and no curve had been allowed for letting a cold wind through. I imagined the trees being placed, one upon the other, notched at both ends to lie flush. There were small squares for windows. The roof was made of the rougher poles to lay the straw upon. Crudely built, perhaps, but it had been a cosy shelter and a sign of the pioneer's independence for it had cost nothing but hard work.

We had bought a small cream separator and when I had milked the goats I carried the pail back to the house. The separator was a marvel of discs and spouts and when it was plugged in it started a great whirring. I poured the milk into the bowl and soon cream trickled from one spout and the separated milk poured from the other. With the cream I made butter and cheese and the milk was for us to share with the baby goats.

The porridge had cooked itself on the embers of the wood stove and I threw in more split wood as Dicky came down dressed ready for school. Robin John, our new baby, was sleeping but he would soon awake and Peter and Susy would help me dress him and play with him, making him gurgle.

On Dicky's first day at his new school I had bundled up the baby and, with Peter and Susy trotting alongside, had walked with him to the top road along our leafy lane, telling him not to be afraid and that it was just like his other school with only two rooms and two teachers. There were other children going along the top road to school and a girl who saw us came over and took Dicky by the hand in a proprietary manner, as country children will, waving me away and telling me that he would 'make out okay' and that she would mind him. She gripped his hand as she herded three other small boys out of the ditch. Looking towards the school I saw other children running out of the bush. I couldn't see a house or a garden gate. They appeared like elves from the woods and Dicky had joined them, beaming at the three elfin boys from the ditch.

By the end of the week he had become an independent schoolboy and, rather than follow the road for two miles, he had found a short-cut across our field and through the bush. He raced away now, banging his lunch-pail and clutching a scribbler. It was his turn, he said, to wear the catcher's mitt.

Each evening after supper Christopher sharpened his axe and went in search of hardwood for fence posts and I cleared bush with my smaller axe. I hacked away between the trees and put the undergrowth in a pile. I felt like a pioneer and said out loud, 'It looks like a park', admiring a few square yards, but to clear all the bush looked impossible. Christopher told me not to worry, when it was time to tackle the tangle of the far bush he would have a chain saw and a tractor. I nodded. I couldn't wander far from the house and children anyway, but where did he get his optimistic attitude? We had had to budget carefully to buy the blooming axe! His visions reached further than mine. We had to have fences and his axe rang through the woods late into the evening. He would finally wander in, too tired to notice the scratches from flying wood or the bites from an army of hungry mosquitoes.

Then one evening he came home looking excited and told me that he was going to buy 'railroad ties' and at once found a pencil and calculated how many he could afford. I stared at him. He wasn't getting the tractor he dreamed of, he was going to build a train! 'Why do you want railroad ties?'

'To make fence-posts with, of course. What do you think, I'm going to build a train? It will save a lot of chopping and also there isn't enough hardwood in the bush for posts. These are already treated, just have to split them.'

He hadn't looked so pleased since he arrived at the

hospital and saw only one baby (the doctor had warned him it might be twins).

'That's good then,' I said, 'but we haven't anything to fence in. The goats never wander far from Nanny when she's tethered.'

'I know,' he went on wisely, 'but we will, one day.'

The goats produced four gallons of milk a day. Jolly, the little doe, was weaned and the male kids we had sold for meat to Europeans. The little white kids were missed. They had infuriated us but still we missed them. We couldn't keep them in the barn, they leaped through the windows or over the half-door and once on the milk-stand they jumped on to the barn roof. If the roof didn't hold them they fell through on to the earth floor or they got stuck on the rafters and we had to get up there and rescue them. When Christopher arrived home they raced to meet him and jumped on the car and did a tap dance. If a car drove in they wanted to tap dance for the people in the car, who didn't always think it was funny. If we stooped down they nibbled our hair and if we sat down they sat next to us. They were like puppies and almost as lovable. So now they had gone, Jolly followed the adult goats to the bush, and there was no more mischief. A little fun went out of our lives and at the same time we sighed with relief.

'I have plenty of butter and cheese and we can't drink all the milk and I hate to bathe in it.'

'We'll feed it to a pig. Have to buy one.'

'We can't. We have to pay the mortgage and we need groceries and other things this month.'

'Okay, we'll get a pig next month.'

We didn't buy a pig the next month, we bought a trailer to pull behind the car. It had flat tyres, a broken tail-light and sides, and looked ready to be thrown away. Christopher thought otherwise.

'It just needs repair. Look, the floor is good, needs new sides. Won't take long to have it shipshape.' He spent several evenings on the trailer and when it was ready he put a hitch on the Austin and took it to bring home the railroad ties. He had built the sides high and he said it would have many good uses, which it did.

He brought home the pigs in the trailer next. We had bought two eight-week-old weanlings, both gilts. One had cost six dollars. It was very small, and the other, a little rounder and longer, cost eight. We put them in the granary and fed them skimmed milk and meal and all the scraps from the kitchen that the dog didn't fancy. We imagined them all growing fat and then having many other little pigs and us getting rich.

I had sold butter and cheese as a health food to several people in Portage and even goat's milk for a baby with infantile eczema who was found to be allergic to cow's milk, so with the money we bought twenty laying hens. We penned them in the good end of the barn and made nest boxes for them. These we imagined laying twenty eggs each day, or maybe, if an off-day, just fifteen, and we would wash them and crate them and grow rich. But, after the excitement of buying them and hearing the farmyard sounds of squeals and grunts and cluck-clucks, we looked at them again and realized we had bought cast-offs.

The smallest gilt was obviously a runt, and the other one had a runny nose. The hens had been sold to make way for plumper, sprightlier hens. These looked as if they had lain themselves ragged. They were moulting, the owner told us, and once they were over that they would be their old selves again. Leghorns, we were told, lay for ever. They had to, we discovered, no one could eat them, they were too tough.

The railroad ties were loaded on to the trailer with the post-hole auger and the spade, and the fence was built. The bush along the farm boundary was cleared back to make a path and, when Christopher had finished, the posts stood in line like a battalion of soldiers ready to march away. We would join them with fencing wire when pay day came.

On Christopher's salary we were fed and clothed and paid the mortgage. If we lived frugally we could find the price of the weanling pigs, the trailer and other farm needs. We were afraid of borrowing. It was still the 'never-never' and then we had no idea how we could repay a loan. We didn't want to get worriedly into debt. So Christopher worked overtime at the garage and then resented the time he had to spend away from the farm. He wanted to do so much for her. Already I saw her as a demanding mistress, and I, his wife, thought of ways to help him. I found a way through a new neighbour.

Up to now our neighbours had been slow to find us and I wasn't sure where they all lived in this wooded area. I didn't intend hunting in the bush for them, I was afraid I would be lost for ever! Yet it was only my imagination. It wasn't long before the Fuller Brush man found us, then the Rawleigh dealer. They were followed by the Jehovah's Witnesses and an encyclopaedia salesman, then a neighbour arrived, the first one. He drove in on his tractor. A weather-beaten farmer with the flat features of a Ukrainian, he wore wide trousers held up by braces and a belt and he brought a gift of apples in two sacks, one inside the other. The kettle was singing on the hearth and I asked him in for tea. Christopher was coming, I told him, he was just finishing cleaning out the pigs. I had a feeling the Ukrainian had just finished cleaning out his pigs too.

I said it was a nice day, to which he answered 'Ya' and silently he removed his black hat and put it under the chair. I fussed with the tea-pot wondering what his name was or if he had told me, and he looked from bushy brows rubbing together horny hands, watching my every movement. As I poured the tea his hand went slowly to his inside jacket pocket. For a moment I had the ridiculous feeling he was reaching for a gun! Instead he brought out a handful of leaflets. They were tracts, and he asked me if I would care to hear the word of The Lord?

When Christopher appeared I hoped we would then gear the conversation away from religion, for religion we considered a personal matter. Not so our farmer. He was out to save us and he considered nothing more important. Christopher couldn't put his mind to a word he said. He was envying his tractor. He did manage to ask, between Deuteronomy 18, 15–18 and Corinthians 12, 28–29 if he preferred a John Deere to a Ford, and when the farmer suggested we should all pray, and bowed his head, Christopher did quickly manage to get in 'How is it for starting in winter?'

I had thought Amos was a bachelor. We were told there were many tucked away in the bush, living a solitary existence, but Amos had a large family. We also learned that he had been a heavy drinker and carouser until his partner in the hayfield had been struck by a bolt of lightning and instantly killed. They said Amos had fallen to his knees and promised then and there never to touch another drop. Then, keeping his word, he married a devout woman, had a large family and took them to church each Sunday in the waggon pulled by the tractor. Cars, he told us, were unnecessary frills, as were the radio and electricity. Some doubted his asceticism, for he readily took a ride in anyone else's car.

My next neighbour came out of the woods. I didn't know where she could possibly live for the trees were thickest in that direction. She looked as if she had spent a life-time there and didn't know what women were wearing these days. Perhaps she was Gretel, grown up. She certainly wasn't Snow White. She was too tall and muscular. She wore a large, loose, hand-knit cardigan that looked like moss, and a heavy skirt to below her knees. On her feet were large, strong rubber boots. She handed me a bunch of rhubarb. I was delighted. It was unusually red and I told her that she must be an exceptionally good gardener to be able to grow such luscious-looking rhubarb in our poor sandy soil.

'I have a large garden and grow everything,' she said sternly. I said that was wonderful, and asked her in for tea.

She sat silently as I made the tea and when I poured, she bowed her head and crossed herself devoutly, making me wish I hadn't let the boys eat the rest of the cake. Desperate for conversation, I remembered the garden and asked her why our corn would not grow. (We had found a patch of soil that had been previously dug so we cultivated it for a few vegetables.)

'It just isn't doing at all well,' I told her.

'At what phase of the moon did you sow?' she asked me.

'The moon?' I stared at her. 'We planted it during the morning.'

'But it still depends on the phase of the moon. You didn't know that?' She looked quite cross at my ignorance. I hung my head.

'Always remember. A full moon for that that grows up and the waning moon for those that grow down. Full for up and low for down.'

'Oh!' I said brightly. 'Like, "when the mites go up the tites go down".' She sat up nervously.

'That's a jingle,' I explained quickly. 'That way you remember that stalactites go down and stalagmites go up. Your saying "Full for up," made me think of it....' She stared at me strangely as I asked her if she'd care for another cup?

I was glad to hear the baby cry for there was silence again. I hurried to him and brought him out smiling, telling her his name. I had done the right thing and we now met on common ground. She took the baby on her knee and bounced him and told me that she was expecting her second baby in the fall and that her five-year-old daughter was going to be happy when she knew. She wasn't telling her until the baby arrived. I was staring in surprise. I had been secretly wondering if she were a nun! Still, I was delighted to have another woman to chat with and we talked babies and the relevant merits of breast-feeding versus the bottle and I was telling her the names and ages of my family, which lasted over a second cup of tea. 'You must be kept very busy,' she said approvingly, handing me back Robin John. I agreed, and told her that her family would be far better spaced than mine and, racing on in my usual 'tell-it-all' way, I complained that there was no really reliable method of family planning. Her mouth set in a grim line and, pulling her cardigan about her, she stood up in her rubber boots. Pointing a finger at me, she quoted with doom in her voice. 'Man shall not cast his seed to the ground,' which made me wonder what she thought we went round doing! She left in a hurry. I was considering calling after her and asking 'then at what phase of the moon should we?'—but I had said enough.

To be truthful, I was finding my new neighbours' proselytizing somewhat formidable. Even the Jehovah's Witness had walked in unannounced and, seeing that I was busy, had quickly held the end of the wet bedsheet which I was struggling to get through the wringer while she read a passage from the Bible held in her other hand. I either strangle myself holding sheets high or they fall, always finding the spot of grease by the wheel, so I was grateful and gave her ten cents for a *Watchtower*. (They have arrived, hot-eyed, ever since.) So when a truck drove into the yard I looked out nervously as a family tumbled out but, laughingly, they called out, 'Hi, neighbour, we're the O'Casys'. I smiled and went to meet them.

I stopped, bedazzled by a sea of laughing blue eyes, while Dicky raced over. They were his friends from the farm he stopped at on the short way home from school. Dee, the mother, looking as young as her daughters, always gave him lemonade. 'It's okay,' she told me, 'he always says thank you.'

The O'Casys told us that they originated from 'Big sky country'. Montana, Dee laughed. They were sheep farmers and Jim O'Casy, tall, lean, squinting under the brim of a cowboy hat, looked born of the drying sun of summer and sharp sting of winter. He ambled stiffly beside Christopher, thinking little of a leg lost in the war, and told him how easily water could be sandpointed and how we could 'fix up' the barn. 'Unless you're airing it that way,' he grinned, turning to look at the roof, and when Christopher said he was going to sharpen the scythe and cut our few acres of hay by hand, he said he would 'pull over' with his mower, when he was through putting up his own hay, so not to worry.

I was ready to talk fundamentals, babies, vegetables and 'the wash', but Dee pushed it aside and at once wanted to know if I would teach dancing. I didn't think she was serious, and how did she know I had taught dancing and of what interest would it be here in the bush?

'Look,' she told me, 'some of us want our kids to learn other things than minding the pigs and hoeing carrots. If you're agreeable we'll try for the school room. I know of other kids who want to learn. You figure out a fee for lessons and I'll see what I can do. Come over some time,' she added before they left. 'I can make a stinger that will knock your eyeballs out!'

I didn't think I would hear more of the dancing class but a few days later Janice, one of the older girls, came racing over Dicky's trail with a message. Dee had written. 'The trustees say the school is not to be used for belly dancing,' she had added. 'If the dough-heads don't know belly from ballet I'm not telling them, we'll let the old devils thrill.' I read it and giggled. I was to know Dee for her forthright manner, added to it a spice of humour. I told Janice I would think of something. We *would* have a dancing class.

It started in the living-room; it wasn't difficult to push what furniture we had against the wall.

Before long, seven little girls would arrive once a week, through the bush and across the field, for their ballet lesson. Using the Grade One R.A.D. ballet record I had ordered from Eaton's, they learned what a plie, a tendú and a port de bras were. They took the unnatural turnout of the hips in their stride and jumped a light jeté and we practised a dance to the record I had. 'Charmaine' was a good start. They wrote their steps carefully in a ballet notebook and they showed imagination acting out mime. We used kitchen chairs for a barre and our ballet shoes were socks.

They were farm kids, going to a country school. They had never heard of Pavlova or Margot Fonteyn and they did not have television to watch. They were bony and tough but beneath it was a natural grace that they could only have observed in the birds' flight or a deer's leap. I saw them learn, without airs, their backs become straighter and their heads held high with an unpretentiousness that made them a joy to teach. I told them they were 'smashing'!

Our fence posts had to continue without wire for now it was September and we needed shelter for our animals, so we 'fixed up' the barn. We pushed in the rotted straw and broken rafters and dragged them out to burn. We searched the bush for tall trees, thick ones for the uprights and lighter poles for the rafters and ceiling. We sank the uprights deep and notched the cross beams and rafters, my job being mainly to hold things and hand up poles. We laid the ceiling, and on this skeleton of poles we put a bed of thick straw. We then put panes of glass in the little square windows and Christopher levelled the barn door. There was no insulation. The animals would have to provide their own by growing thick coats this winter. It was a shelter. It would be dry and windproof, and it had cost nothing but hard work.

Jim O'Casy then asked us what we were going to do come 'freeze up'? 'The last bachelor who had wintered on your place had his provisions dropped off on the top road and he snow-shoe'd out for them and snow-shoe'd back with them.' Jim's eyes always twinkled when he related a story, so we were never sure if he was pulling our leg, but we knew our lane, our leafy 'English' lane. It could be blocked solid by snowfall. We closed our eyes and prayed it wouldn't happen, and then determinedly tried not to think about it.

TWELVE

DANCING LESSONS AND A CHRISTMAS CONCERT

My dancing class grew, from the living-room at home to a studio in town. The Allied Arts Council wanted to add ballet to its list of classes offered and I was asked to teach. When I told Dee that I couldn't possibly teach ballet, run a home and help start a farm, she said 'Nonsense, of course you can.' Dee was ahead of her time on women's liberation. She thrived on new interests and occupations, and she encouraged it in her daughters. My favourite O'Casy dancer was later to take up wrestling, win a few bouts, and then take a book-keeping course and work in an office. The last we heard, she was thinking of being a 'Mountie' now they were accepting women!

'On Saturdays you could leave the children here while you take my girls and teach in town,' she offered, and it worked well. I also taught Thursday evening, but then Christopher was at home to take care of things while I packed leotard and ballet shoes. I was paid by cheque at the end of each month. They would have been amazed at what the ballet mistress bought with the money!

When we realized how much grain we had to buy to feed the sows and the hens, we knew we had made a mistake. There were few eggs left to sell after we had used them for meals and the sows were growing larger and hungrier. We also felt a responsibility towards them and bought many bags of feed to keep them satisfied. We said to each other, hopefully, that the sows would have babies and we would sell them and regain our losses that way, and meanwhile we kept going to the mill for another bag of feed.

With our intention of starting a Jersey herd, and now

another pay cheque coming in, we felt ambitious and visited a Jersey breeder who lived north of Portage, hoping to buy a heifer calf. There are few Jersey cattle breeders in Manitoba. Most farmer consider them too delicate to withstand the cold climate. This we found wasn't so. Young growing stock grow thick coats if they are outside and the dairy cows in the barn require only the same attention as other dairy cows, and for the small farmer they require less room and eat less food.

Mr Adams had a large herd and we had visited him before, mainly to admire them. They were golden, sleek and good producers. He knew we wanted to start a herd and he thought we should start with the best and offered us two heifer calves. Peter at once named them. Dicky had named the sows, we reminded him (though we didn't often call them Pip and Squeak!). Peter chose Peewee for one calf and Susy named the other Bambie. We brought them home in the back seat of the warm car, their tail ends in sacks and their heads cradled by three loving children.

There was no snow as yet but the ground was granite hard and we kept all the animals in the barn for warmth. The hens were penned at the south end and the sows solidly penned between the calves and the goats. There was still plenty of room with the hay stacked at the north end, with the barrels for meal and oats, and on one side the bales of straw for bedding.

We bought the Jersey calves with my first pay cheque and, soon after, Mr Adams offered us to two cows to start our herd. One was a heifer, due to have her first calf in January, and the other was an older cow, good for a few more calves. Both came from a long line of high butter-fat producers and he had the old cow's milk record to prove it. We were excited. It was the dream beginning to take shape, but I would have to put in many more hours of ballet to buy both of them, so Mr Adams said we could 'buy them on time'.

With the extra pay cheque we thought it now safe to do this. I said that mine should be used exclusively for cows, as Christopher's cheque was already carefully budgeted. This was decided and Mr Adams said he would bring the cows in his truck the next day. We all went down to the barn to welcome them.

Eve jumped down first. She looked very self-assured and let Christopher lead her to the barn, and she dipped her head to us like the Queen. In time she did become the queen of the herd and reigned for sixteen years! Betty, with soft brown eyes, blinking at the sunlight, followed slowly. She was tied in the barn and she let the children hug her and feel her crumpled horn. When I came home from my dancing class the next evening I found Robin John and Susy nestled in the hay while Dicky and Peter were handing nails and boards to daddy who had built standings for Eve and Betty. He had proper chain tie-ups and mangers in front of them, and above them, their names were printed in large, important letters.

We should have bought a comfortable chair for the living-room, better clothes, an oil furnace, but we couldn't let the goal be side-tracked. It would have been cheating, we felt, and we decided we didn't desperately need those things.

Our furniture was adequate for the time being. We were warm enough even if it did mean chopping wood and lugging it in by the basketful. I didn't like the L-shaped stove pipes that led to the bedrooms and heated them. I had to dust them regularly, but we were compensated by the smell of a wood fire and the comforting crackles from the stove in the kitchen and the Quebec heater we sat around. We had beaten the elements by our own means, we didn't call for help, and that was independence.

But we couldn't be all independent. Many things had to be bought, rice, flour, sugar, gas for the car, feed for the animals. There was little left for extras, because there were birthdays and we always bought gifts, however small. We had set the rules from the start. Of course I needed towels and a new iron, but not for my birthday. I wouldn't buy Christopher work gloves or socks. It had to be 'a non-necessity'. A plant in a pot for me, a paperback for him, and something special for the children.

There were three birthdays in October. Dicky's came first and we bought him a sketch pad and pencils for he was already showing the beginnings of the artist he was to eventually become, but for our birthdays, Christopher's and mine, that were next, we added a new rule. We would give each other a gift, but it mustn't cost money!

I furrowed my brow over something for him, and my own arrived while I was wondering if I should bake him a cake with ingredients from the cupboard or unravel an old scarf and knit him a toque. On the 13th, my birthday, he left in a hurry, grinning. He kissed me on top of the head, because he is taller, and said I would have to be patient and wait until evening.

I wondered what he was up to. Had he taken my ballet shoes to the garage and was secretly darning them (the toes were wearing thin)? Maybe he was fashioning a bowl from an old hubcap. I sat feeling sorry for myself. I really wanted a proper gift, something posh. I was tired of stinting and saving, making ends meet and doing without. Then I felt ashamed. If I worked hard, he worked even harder and he didn't complain. I thought of all the things he would want to have if he could. I didn't want anything. I was so fortunate I had him, I had the children, and anyway, I had made the crazy new rule. He came home with something under his coat and he at once told me to sit down and hold out my arms.

'Hold it tight. Open your eyes!'

I did. I gasped. I was cuddling a small black cocker spaniel puppy and it was licking my hand. I wanted to laugh, and I was crying at the same time. We loved dogs, especially cocker spaniels, but we knew we couldn't own one. They were just handsome dogs we could pat if we saw one and admire pictures of, while continuing to fondle old Deena's ears and giving a meal to other mutts who wandered to the farm.

The children were whooping with joy and saying they knew it was arriving and it had been awfully hard to keep the secret and Susy was rolling on the floor in her eagerness to hold the pup. I looked up at Christopher. 'You bought it.

You cheated,' I said. 'She's purebred. Look at her ears and her face. She's a purebred dog, purebred dogs are expensive.'

'No, I didn't buy it,' he said quickly, 'Aggie told me about it. Reverend Morman is going on a mission to China and he wanted a home for the pup. I knew you'd like a cocker spaniel puppy.'

'Like it, her. I love her, and,' I said, wiping my eyes, 'I feel like a millionaire. What are we going to call her?'

We spent all evening trying out names and decided on Cindy. She was soon one of the family but I was still with the dilemma of what to give Christopher for his birthday, so I phoned Aggie. 'Isn't that funny,' she said at once. 'I was going to phone you today. Reverend Morman was wondering if you would like Tippy too. That's the pup's mother. They leave in a few days and haven't had time to find a home for her.'

On Christopher's birthday I drove him to work and said I needed the car for groceries and as soon as he was gone we bought a loaf of bread and went and got Tippy. When Christopher got home I told him to sit down and close his eyes, but Tippy had heard him arrive and came galomping down the stairs barking. She had met Christopher but she hadn't seen her pup for a while, so she gave him a 'Hi there' look and ran to rescue Cindy who was rolling on the floor with Susy, they were so excited.

We didn't know at the time and Aggie didn't know what she had started, but it was Tippy who opened up a whole new area in our life in later years.

A few evenings later Christopher watched me dip water out of the pail and said he was going down to the basement. 'I'm going to dig for water,' he told me. I nodded. I didn't think he would find any but we didn't have TV and there was nothing on radio.

The basement was a bricked up dug-out with an earth floor. I heard the spade slice into the sand and soon he came up, went outside and came in with the post-hole auger and a pipe speckled with holes, pointed at one end.

'Going to wham the sandpoint in and see what happens.'

I continued putting Robin John to bed and telling Susy to keep away from the basement stairs.

'Going to pump water now. Want to see?' He called up. The children were behind me and we all went down to watch. He had screwed on a small hand pump and was pumping vigorously. He primed it with water from a jug and pumped again. A small trickle of orange-coloured water coughed its way up. He mopped his brow. 'I know there is water down there. Think I'll phone Jim.'

We had had the telephone installed soon after we moved to the farm, a necessity, we thought, in the country. It was a hand-cranked wall phone with a separate earphone and we shared a party line with a dozen other people. He asked if the line was busy and then gave the four hand cranks for the O'Casy ring. Jim was home. He listened to the problem and said he would be right over.

He followed Christopher with one leg leading stiffly and I heard them talking and digging and finally they came up carrying the sandpoint. 'The holes in the sandpoint are too fine. I have to get another size. Then it will work.' I wasn't so hopeful.

The next evening we watched him bore holes in my kitchen cupboard; a water pipe was brought from the sandpoint, the hand pump screwed on again and he pumped eagerly. It coughed, then a splutter and at last a swish, soon water was pouring out, cold and clear. Christopher stood back to our applause.

'Guess what else I'm going to do?'

I looked at him wide-eyed. 'I've no idea,' I said, and I didn't think I could take another miracle so soon.

'I'm going to put a pipe from the sink and bore a hole in the wall so that we can run the water out, as well as in. What do you think of that?'

I frowned. 'The ground is frozen. It will freeze in the pipe.'

'Ah!' He shook a finger. 'Not if I slant it down. I'll pipe it out of the way. It will make a skating rink for the boys. Dicky keeps on about one.'

The first real snowfall gave us an anxious moment. Were

we to be snowed in all winter? But the snow fell gently in the bush, a soft carpet of snow. It seemed a sacrilege to mar its beauty, but our livelihood depended on us getting to town, so Christopher drove the car up and down the lane to make a trail. The road had to be clear for the teachers to follow as well, for I had said I would help with the Christmas concert.

I had already considered the country school teacher a special breed but when I saw how they handled a two-room school my admiration grew. These teachers had stamina, courage and a good sense of humour. They needed it. They weren't sure what made them renew their contract and stay three years. They drove out from town and in winter the roads were slippery. They forgot the number of times they were snowbound and walked part of the way, and in summer there were the woodticks.

I heard about the woodticks when Dicky came home and said he had the highest score. I thought he had done well in arithmetic until he told me that he was the boy with the most woodticks! The teachers had made them put a jar on their desk and put the woodticks in it. They were small bugs that clung to the children as they raced through the bush and if they stayed on them they dug under and would swell up on blood. The jars were to keep the woodticks off the floor. There wasn't a janitor.

The teacher, along with the help of an older boy, unplugged the toilets and stoked the furnace. It was more than a school. It was a family. She shared their problems and appreciated their maturity. If she couldn't start her car at four, there was always a lad in Grade Eight who would look under the hood and get it running for her. She didn't raise her eyebrows when one of the girls brought her baby sister to school. She knew the mother was in hospital and dad was in the field haying.

The town teacher might have thought the country boy hopelessly dense in school, but she took her car to the garage and didn't know his other abilities, and babies aren't allowed in the classroom in town schools. Their values were different. They couldn't understand Keats or Shelley but they would carefully shoo a baby skunk across the road before a car came and ran it over, and they wouldn't harm a garter snake (though they might put it in the teacher's desk!).

The Christmas concert in the country was the highlight of the year but this was our teachers' last. One was getting married and the other wanted to teach nearer home, so they wanted it to be their best.

We were a 'mixed lot' in the bush. The district was called Gainsborough, named by the first settlers in honour of the English painter. Perhaps the trembling, leafy poplars did resemble the artist's work, but few people in the district were of English descent. North, over the river, in the Macdonald district, they were for the most part Scottish of origin, and to the south in St Claude they were nearly all French. Hidden in the Gainsborough bush were those who could claim Ukrainian, Indian, Irish and French heritages, not that the children cared. They ran up the Canadian flag each morning and were as one. The adults weren't so sure. Their backgrounds didn't spring from the same roots and then I came along and caused added friction.

I had chosen six little girls for a highland fling and they learned the new steps quickly, but we had no sooner learned it when the teacher came over and drew me aside. 'Not the two on the left,' she whispered. 'Jehovah's Witnesses.'

I chose two other girls to take their place and she stopped me again. 'Not the one on the right,' she told me. 'Plymouth Brethren.'

The trustees arrived the next day. They were local farmers and they had been cleaning out the barn and were annoyed at being called away. They said that this 'belly dancing' was not to go on in school hours. Readin', writin', and 'rithmetic was what the school was for. The teachers asked if we could continue at noon? The teachers explained to me later that the girls had been dancing in school hours while they had been teaching letters to the Grade Ones.

So we continued. One teacher would come for me at noon and, despite the dissensions from the district, the children enjoyed the break from routine and the Ukrainian teacher said she had never seen the Kolamaka danced with such spirit. The teachers also thought it was better they were dancing in the school than sneaking to the horse barn to do 'God knows what!' The children who were not allowed to be in the concert looked after my children while we practised (though I had a strong feeling they would rather have been learning the Irish jig).

On the night of the concert we had our first real snowstorm and I wondered if it would all have to be cancelled. I thought of all the work: the lunches the teachers had eaten on the run, the costumes Dee and other mothers had so carefully made, the yards of ribbon sewn on skirts, the cossack hats and head-dresses we had fashioned for the dancers. We looked at the tight lace curtain of snow and decided to try anyway. We scraped the frost from the windshield and travelled the country way, invented by Canadians determined to get where they wanted to go. Forging ahead, shovelling furiously, backing up and forging ahead through snowdrifts, shovelling again, backing up, tearing ahead, we reached the top road in a cloud of steam and Christopher in his shirt sleeves, sweating.

They must have all come the Canadian way. The school yard was filling up with trucks and cars and people were already kicking off snow at the door. We went in and found seats and I held Robin John, anxious to be backstage dressing my dancers and giving them encouragement.

'I should be at the back.' Christopher reached up for Robin John but the woman in the next seat took him. 'Go ahead, missus, the baby will be fine with me. First Christmas I haven't had a little 'un on my lap, don't seem right. All my kids are back there.' She jerked her head to the curtains, sheets dyed red, glittering with silver stars at the top.

'Thanks. If he is a bother, Christopher can hold him.'

'Naw, dads are no good at holding babies. Say, the bally dress sure looks cute on my little Darleen. she was primpin' around all last evening in it.'

I stared at her. This stout, heavy-featured woman was

the mother of the daintiest child I had taught. She was dancing the solo in a Christmas ballet that I had taught the smallest girls. 'Darleen is a natural. I wish she could continue her dancing. She's a talented girl.' Robin John was pulling the babuska off the woman's head. She squeezed him and held him up to see the decorations.

'Naw,' she snorted at me. 'Her dad wouldn't want her jumping around on her toes, getting silly ideas. Plenty enough to do at home without that stuff!' She looked at me warningly.

I dressed the ballerinas nervously, my hands shaking. I had been asked to help and I was encouraged by Dee. 'Let's give them a bit of culture,' she said defiantly, 'other than agri! Be a change from carrying in wood and slopping the pigs.' But I had felt a breath of disapproval at my interference, an undercurrent!

I had felt it when the trustees had arrived, bushy-browed, staring at the dancing. I had felt it in the notes sent to the teachers excusing children from the concert. I had felt it from the parents who didn't care what they did, 'but who did she think she was, expecting us to make costumes for a stupid dance!'

'I think we had better get started,' the Ukrainian teacher whispered. Her hands were shaking as much as mine. We could hear the 'back row boys' chanting. They were singing un-Christmassy songs and stamping their feet. I had seen them when I came in. They had kept their coats on, looking as if they had just come in to get out of the cold but once there decided to stay and enjoy themselves. One had called out and winked at me. Now he was singing the loudest. Dee said he did this at all the concerts, and at dances he danced by himself, but he was no bother for when things really got started he would be asleep under the bench.

Chairs scraped back as the older teacher struck up on the piano and the curtains opened to the welcome from the lower grades. The school was hushed to silence.

I lined up my ballerinas while the master of ceremonies announced the next item, adding a joke or two to entertain. The jokes became less mild as he nipped outside and warmed to his work.

I had only seen the children in trousers and workaday shirts. I beamed with pride at my little dancers. They were transformed! Their tutus stood out stiffly and their satin tops shone. They were scraps of net from ancient dance dresses and satin blouses and slips cut down, all from Dee's and other mothers' workbaskets. For ballet shoes they had clean white socks.

I lined up the Ukrainian dancers as the Christmas play ended, smoothing the ribbons on the French-Canadian girl's head-dress and pushing the Indian boy's cossack hat down firmly. They sprang on to the stage, knees high, ribbons flying, keeping in time with the fast beat of the music. They finished, flushed and panting, and I thought the applause could have lasted longer. The kids had danced their hearts out.

The Irish jig and highland fling were separated by verse from the Grade Fives, then there was the Nativity and the carols. It all ended with a cold Santa, with real snow on his suit, pushing his way in thankfully after standing outside ringing the sleigh bells while the M.C. built up the anticipation.

The oranges and candy were handed out after the gifts, and no one was forgotten. (The children not allowed in the concert had had their gifts that morning.) The women's group had the tin urn ready and went up and down the rows filling mugs with steaming coffee, followed by trays of sandwiches. The crowd departed, with a little old lady at the door, handing out tracts with a gentle 'God bless you'. The teachers sat on the edge of the stage, weak with relief and exhaustion. They hadn't left the school that day for fear of being snowbound and now they wondered if it had all been worth the effort.

I felt a let-down too. The weeks of preparation, the doubts about its success, and now a bare tree and orange peel on the floor and snow that had turned to puddles at the door.

We heard later that horses had been hitched to cars stranded in wood trails. Some had walked to the concert, but no one had stayed away. Not a line was forgotten or a step tripped up on. They had complained and grumbled, but they knew it was important that they get there. They knew it was worth it.

Later the teachers would go to town school and teach and never again would they become so involved or so important to their pupils. The last stronghold in the country would be events only remembered with nostalgia.

THIRTEEN

BILLS, THE BUSH AND BETTY

Living in the bush in winter was like living inside a Christmas card, one which had the snow falling gently and the trees bowed down with the stuff. Added to this, our bush had a jay bird, blue as the Canadian sky. He came for his rations each day and frightened away the chickadees.

We had banked the skating rink with snow and I had to remember not to run water away when they were skating! Dicky could hit a puck with his hockey stick while Susy pushed a chair around learning to keep her balance. Peter kept falling and he came in before the others. He preferred to play with Robin John or quietly push his cars along. Then he took his first seizure.

I had never seen a 'grand mal' epileptic seizure and I was always to be thankful that Christopher was home that day. We rushed him to hospital, I holding him close while Christopher shovelled out the snowy lane and the other children were huddled in the back for warmth.

Again we had to learn that courage was not wailing or fighting against adversity and injustice, but waiting, doing the chores, listening to the other children's chatter. So difficult to do cheerfully when your heart is filled with fear. When he came home, it was with a prescription for a daily medication and the knowledge that Peter, our second son, was retarded.

I couldn't accept it. We would give him the medication for his seizures but I didn't think he would need it for long. We watched him steady his baby brother when he stumbled. We saw him play, laugh and fight, no different from any five-year-old. I refused to think he was different. I was the same as any other mother who wanted her child to be like other children, good at school, loved and accepted. I bought him a story book with lots of pictures and read to him slowly, praying he would understand, and learn.

Eve had a heifer calf. It was born late at night and we stayed with her for the birth. Eve washed her with a brisk tongue as if she knew it was twenty degrees below zero outside and it was important to keep the baby warm. Christopher set up the heat lamp in the pen and we then dried the calf under it. Not wanting to leave the lamp without attention in the log barn, I then put a sweater on her. It was the same sweater we had put on Bambie when she first slept in the cold barn. The English grandmas always sent hand-knitted 'woollies' and these had been well worn by the children. I didn't think they would mind this new use for them and Mum always said that wool was best next to the skin.

Betty's calf arrived a week later. Another heifer. We couldn't believe our luck. We dried her too under the lamp and put on her the other sweater, the one Peewee had worn. I named Betty's calf Sunflower, and Christopher, not to be outdone, named Eve's Sunshine.

Before long the sows gave birth to eleven piglets between them. We soon didn't know who's was who but we were then buying bags of meal for pigs there was no market for and were told were not worth raising. We looked at our folly uneasily and dished out more gruel for their hungry mouths.

The goats then had their kids. Six soft noses pushed at us, bleating their baby cries. The barn was full now of tender, throbbing, hungry life and the trailer behind the car was never arriving home without a load of oats, meal or hay.

We were selling cream. The milk from the two cows and four goats half-filled the cream can and Christopher would deliver it on his way to work. We waited eagerly for the cream cheques. The first four were just enough to pay for the last month's feed bill. The oats and hay would have to wait for the next cheque.

However quietly we entered the barn the pigs would deafen us by their squeals for more food and the hens came running for another pecking of grain. The calves and kids wanted meal and soft hay and the cows wanted hay and oats. We knew we had to sell them to cut down the food costs.

'Some farmers have killed off their litters. They say they aren't worth raising with the prices so low.' Christopher brought home this news and I shook my head worriedly.

'It seems so wrong. Could the market change in a month or so? They say it's a fluctuating one.'

'No, it won't increase, not until the farmers go out of the business and stop raising pigs. Then they'll put on a subsidy to coax them back in. It's not stable enough, and the small farmer is the hardest one hit. Let's advertise them, or give them away. Anything to save me facing the feed mill with promises again.'

It wasn't the right time for the car to abandon us, but it did. It seemed the little Austin wasn't taking any more ploughings into snowbanks and fast back-ups. We had just finished paying for it and when it was really ours, it breathed its last, so we took off the trailer hitch and traded it for an old 'Chevvy'. Scratched and dented, the old Chevvy roared through the snow like a wild bull and used twice as much gas to run. We didn't like it. Sitting in it we felt like a gang of wild Indians and it had a hollywood muffler that we had to do something about. On top of that, we had to juggle the budget to buy the horrible car!

The expenses piled up. The animals were hungrier than ever (though I thought they looked better than we did) and winter had given way to spring which had arrived without us noticing. The sun was making puddles in the yard and a week later robins gathered in the field. The snow receded to the far bush, redstarts flittered brightly and patches of wet grass grew larger each afternoon.

I had waited so long for warmth, a bone-warming benign sunshine, our reward for enduring winter, and now I was too distracted by our mounting bills to notice. The pussy-willows burst forth at the edge of the bush. I shouldn't have missed them; then I walked right by a clump of violets. Dicky pointed them out and picked me a posy. My heart warmed, but the burden of unpaid bills blinded me. The dream had become a nightmare.

We sold the weanlings for six and a half dollars and two runts for five. The sows went to market and they brought us in a cheque for seventy-five dollars. Many of the hens had not wintered well. Some of the silly ones had jumped out in the snow and returned with frozen toes and wattles. We had a recipe for canning old hens, so we spent several gory evenings chopping off heads and plucking them behind the barn, then we cut them up and pushed the parts into sealers and the fire roared as we steamed them for hours. The six best hens, who had started to lay eggs as if their lives depended on it (and they did), had fresh straw put in their nest boxes and they scratched in the sunshine and breathed easier. The goat kids were getting out again and charming us with their mischievous ways.

But the animals that we had arranged to come into the world were not meant to charm and create a pretty picture, to prance among the trees and be there to be patted and played with. They were there to fatten and kill. We sold the kids for meat to the same Europeans, but they were the last goats we were to raise for meat.

Farming was a business, we knew. Killing was a part of it. These were the hard facts. It was why we wanted the dairy to be our way of farming. We wanted our animals to roam among the trees and create a pretty picture, to lap up the clover and be patted. The raising of animals for meat alone and the decision of life or death would have to be for more knowledgeable hands than ours.

The grass was green and sun-warmed that Easter, and Peter started school. We bought him a new jacket and a bright yellow lunch pail, and he had a note about taking his noon medication (that was in a small bottle and in the teacher's care). He looked so eager and I watched him race with Dicky across the field. At four o'clock I waited for the teacher to dismiss the class and then I asked her how Peter was at school. It was the young teacher's first school. Dicky told us after the first week that she was 'all right'.

She read them stories and they learned a prayer and if the children were rough or used bad language she looked sad, and once she had cried. I don't think they had seen a teacher cry before and after that they were careful not to hurt her feelings. I heard that the older boys were combing their hair and washing their faces, for Miss Freisen was pretty and no taller than they were. They kept all their mischief for the other teacher, who had taught at three other schools and kept a strap in her drawer.

'Peter settled in very well,' Miss Freisen told me softly. 'He is a quiet little fellow. We did printing and colouring. He enjoyed the colouring but he found the printing difficult so I let him play with the Plasticine. I don't rush them the first day. He had a sleep in the afternoon. It's quite a new experience for him.'

'Does he mix well?' I wanted to hear that he played on the swing and kicked a ball and I didn't want to hear if he had fallen.

'Just fine. It is his first day and he was shy of course, but he will adjust, I am sure,' she said gently.

'You really think so? He will?' It was what I wanted to hear. I could have hugged her. He was going to be all right, just like any ordinary little boy.

We couldn't get on top of our pile of bills. The hay wasn't paid for, nor the oats. We needed fencing wire. We needed a tractor, a manure spreader (there was a small mountain in front of the barn). We needed many things to make the bush a farm, and we could just pay the mortgage. Something else would have to go, and we both thought of Betty.

Betty was dry. She was an elderly cow and her lactations were short and we had had a fine heifer calf from her.

'I guess she will have to go to market.' Christopher found it hard to say. She had been the start of the dream.

'We barely had enough for the mortgage. There's nothing else.' I turned away. I felt like 'Jack and the Beanstalk's' mother, only I hoped he wouldn't bring back a handful of beans. With our luck they wouldn't grow!

We paid part of our bills and bought some fencing wire when we sold Betty. The grass was growing. We were putting the animals in the east bush first and we started to clear the undergrowth in earnest. My dancing class had ended with the season and my time was more free and the evenings longer.

On the next weekend we decided to spend all our time in the bush. The children would mind Robin John and even help a little. We were following the pioneer custom, not much money but plenty of work clearing the land.

Saturday came cool and pleasant. I filled the picnic basket with weiners and marshmallows for the bonfires and went ahead with my small axe while Christopher sharpened his and the children stayed to play a game they had just invented.

I strolled into the bush wondering where the goats and calves were. They usually ran to meet me. I went further and there was a hollow, and there I saw Peewee. I walked up to her. She was flat out and her eyes were sunken. She was dead. I looked round for the other animals but they were nowhere. Christopher had come up behind me and he bent down. He felt her cold body and turned her over. I looked on, numb with grief. We had had to sell Betty, now this. Was there no end?

'Where are the rest of the animals?'

'I don't know. They usually stay together.'

'Walk that way round and I'll go the other. Call if you see them.'

I followed the cow trail to the fence line, peering into the deeper bush where a Jersey blended imperceptibly into the light and shade and the yellows of the foliage. I hadn't looked far when I heard a shrill whistle from the other side of the bush. I ran towards the sound, praying the other animals were alive.

I saw the goats. Annabelle was reaching for a leaf and maa'd a greeting. I touched her and Christopher was watching Eve and the two small calves.

'These are okay, but Bambie is walking stiffly, as if she can't see. I'm going to phone the vet. I want you to look around the barn, everywhere, see if they could have got at anything. Paint, battery fluid. Search!' He ran ahead and I went by the barn to meet the children who were on their way with the picnic basket.

I opened my mouth to tell them to stay in the yard. To go back, away. That daddy and I were busy, then I thought of all the things we had been through together. The joy of moving to the farm. Finding the water. The skating rink. The sorrows. Peter's illness. Losing Cindy when the tree fell on her. The striving and saving and going without. Not having the parkas with the fur inside but the cheaper ones and having to wear grandma's woollies under, for the extra warmth. They hadn't complained, they had understood somehow, our hopes and ambitions.

'Peewee is dead,' I told them bluntly. 'Daddy thinks it could be a poison of some kind. We want you to search around and see if there is any paint, or anything that an animal might get at.'

Susy was crying. She had loved Peewee best. Peewee let her feel her nose and the funny parts of her neck until Bambie pushed her gently away so it could be her turn. The boys had raced off, on their important mission. I followed slowly.

I didn't think there could be anything around the yard. I was sure. To protect the children we never left lids off anything they could possibly put a finger in and taste, so the animals were protected as well.

'The vet is on his way,' Christopher came out and told me. 'Did you search?'

'Of course. We all looked,' I said irritably. 'There's nothing.'

'I guess it could be something they ate in the bush. I'll wait here to take him out,' he told me.

'We might as well go to the bush. The kids are getting the basket.' I went on sadly.

The vet was able to save Bambie and he had Peewee opened up and samples were taken and sent away to Winnipeg. The conclusion was that the cow had most likely died from eating a poisonous weed or plant.

We went through the bush. Wiry willows snapped at us as we pushed through. It was a denizen of natural growth—bluebells, golden rod, wild asters, wood orchid. Could they harm? We didn't think so. There was a patch of wild strawberries. I picked them, but there were so many broad-leaf plants, some white-veined, and there was fungus. Christopher kicked at a fleshy toadstool bitterly. He was going to destroy the menace, open the darkest corner to the sun.

We cleared bush each evening and at the weekend we went to burn the piles. We took dry straw and old oil, pushed the straw into the heart of the brush pile and lit a match. It was a windless day. As one pile burned down we lit another until there was a circle of beacons, smelling pleasantly of log fires and weiner roasts. The bonfires burned well. Red and yellow flames leaped to the branches of the trees, but their leaping was short-lived and died before they reached the trees. All the same we watched carefully. The air was dry and the breeze, in gusts, encouraged the flames. Looking up, we didn't see the fingers of flame creep away, burst open at a clump of twigs and dead leaves. Other avenues spread and one set on fire a large, partly dead bush. We then tried to put them out but there were too many. They had got out of control and we looked in panic as they now raced towards the fence and our neighbour's land.

'Run and get pails of water and sacks,' Christopher commanded, trying to keep his voice steady. Smoke was rising from his boots as I left him stamping at the flames.

I called the children to stay in the yard and not to follow. I didn't want them out there trapped in the beacons of fire. I hurried back with full pails and sacks over my head and water splashing down my pants. Christopher ran to help me and we soaked the sacks and slapped furiously at the spreading flames.

We worked frantically and had no idea for how long, but Christopher was pouring water on a fence post charred by the fire when he saw Jim on his tractor, the other side of the fence, grinning down at us. 'Getting tired of swinging the axe, eh?' Christopher looked sheepish and tried to grin back.

'Fire got a bit out of hand, thought we'd better stop it.'

We were coal black. Our hair was singed. I felt a crisp strand with my fingers and Christopher had torn his shirt. Exhausted, we felt we had just quelled a major forest fire.

'Well, I brought the plough in case we needed a fire guard, but you got her out. Should have let her burn and got rid of all your underbush and you could have slapped it out at the fence line. A lot of it would have hit a damp spot and put itself out anyway.'

'Yeah. I thought of that,' Christopher said airily. 'But the axe can do the rest. No trouble.'

I smiled at Jim and agreed with Christopher, and waited until we reached home to kick him.

We bought more fencing wire and moved the cow and calves to another pasture. Bambie was a grown heifer but we still thought of her as a calf. She had mooed plaintively for Peewee, her buddy, her little sister. We missed Peewee too, but we missed Betty more. We thought of the milk she had given in her lifetime. She was old but she was gentle. She had given us Sunflower, and she could have given us more calves. The foundation of her herd, and we had sent her for slaughter. Then Christopher came home from work and sat down rubbing his face, looking as if he had seen a ghost.

'I saw Betty today.'

I stared at him. He was looking straight ahead and he didn't look at me. I quickly made him a cup of hot, sweet tea, as they say in the first-aid books, and knew I must keep him calm. He was breaking down. The damn farm was the cause.

'Did you hear what I said?'

'Yes, dear, that was nice. I sometimes see my father and he's been dead . . . how long?'

He gulped down the tea and stood up. 'I knew you wouldn't believe me. Call me when supper's ready. I'm going to take a load of manure out with the car and trailer. Ruddy car roars like a tractor, might as well use it as one.'

Betty wasn't mentioned again until the next evening. 'Well, I saw Betty again. Spoke to her this time.'

I rushed for the tea-pot. It was the worry of the farm. He was mad, completely mad.

'You don't believe me, do you? You think I'm mad. A regular basket case.' He stood up and gripped me by the hand. 'Okay, come with me. It's not far, just a mile or so. Call the kids. Come on.'

I called the children and we got into the car. I smiled bravely and told them that daddy was taking us for a little ride. 'Daddy is off his rocker,' I wanted to tell them. 'We must all humour him, and hold on to each other.'

But daddy was looking very sane. We were taken towards town and he stopped at a farm where there was a railed-in feed-lot where he stopped the car and beckoned us to follow. There were Herefords and some mixed breeds eating, with their backs to us at the racks of hay. Then I saw that pressed between them was a small brown cow. Christopher whistled and called and the cow turned around and hurried over to us. I saw the liquid brown eyes and the crumpled horn and I gasped. Soon Betty was licking my face, wet with tears.

'It is Betty. How did you know?' We were lifting the children up so they could pat her.

'Well, several times, as I drove home, I thought I saw a Jersey among the steers here and when I was sure I slowed down, but then I drove on. I thought I was seeing things. Then the next day she was at the rail looking at me so I stopped and came and looked at her. She mooed and licked me and I saw her crumpled horn. Anyway I went and saw the farmer. He said he had bought her in a lot of four sold together.'

'Could we buy her back?'

'I asked him. He doesn't care. Jerseys don't fatten, he said. So if I give him what he paid for her. . . .'

My mind raced. Where could we get the eighty-five dollars to buy her back? It was a second chance. Things like this didn't happen often. If we had Betty our herd would get going again. Fate (or was it God) had sent her back to us to try again. Now he was putting us to the test of getting her back again. Oh, God, you do try us so!

'I went to the bank today.'

I looked up from laying the table. Christopher was fondling Tippy's ears and getting comfort from her adoring gaze.

'He wanted to know what collateral we had,' he went on.

'What's that?'

'What we own. The stuff we have.' He let Tippy out to run. 'I told him and he suggested we sold the place and moved to town.'

I thought about the bank manager, sitting behind his desk as Christopher told him about the goats and calves, hiding a smile behind a soft white hand, perhaps trying not to laugh.

But Christopher would have said it with love in his eyes. He would have wanted to tell him about Betty, but a bank manager wouldn't have understood. He had never seen the foaming pail of milk and the soft muzzle. He had never caught the blossoms from the bush, seen the oriole weave her swinging nest with such faith. He didn't know about the hard work, the dream, and how it all held us bound to a commitment. The farm was ours. It was accepting us, and we had promises to keep.

The next day I took Christopher to work so that I could use the car, which I did when there were things to get home, shopping to do, but today I wasn't going shopping. I was going to get a job.

I had heard that nurse's aides were needed at the Home

for Retarded Children in Portage. I didn't want to leave the children during the day so I was going to see if I could get a night-time job. I was interviewed, fitted for a uniform, given a physical and told I would be phoned when they needed me. I was to have the midnight duty, and I was called in to work two days later.

From the solitude of the farm, I marched into a world of sights and smells that would sicken me, a world of sadnesses and sorrows that would haunt my dreams and give me the most bizarre six months of my life.

FOURTEEN

HOSPITAL INTERLUDE

I pulled on the blue dress and caught my chin on the stiff white bib, then I was handed a white cloth band.

'Pull it around your waist tight and pin it. That keeps your bib down.' The supervisor was telling me how to wear the uniform of a nurse's aide. I next put on a starched white apron. It billowed around and buttoned at the back. I felt I was a demure sight in blue and white and below were my black stockings and sensible black, rubber-soled shoes.

'You are to work in the New Unit,' the supervisor told me. 'Come along.'

I followed her across a courtyard. From another building I could hear strange, high-pitched cries, and I caught the odour of soiled beds. The supervisor didn't speak but she did turn round to see if I was still there, and hadn't fled away in terror.

Four black-caped nurses marched by, two abreast. We stood to one side as they went by. It looked military. A changing of the guard. I followed on to the ward office where two other nurses were removing their capes and showing their smart uniforms and I wondered, now I was wearing my own pretty uniform, what would I have to do?

I was introduced to the two nurses I was to help. The supervisor had told them I was new, but I thought I should add that I wasn't really a nurse. I had never worked in a hospital before, though I didn't think I would have to handle the forceps or anything. Miss Weibe, the head nurse, smiled gently and told me not to worry, that the duties were quite ordinary. I thought, couldn't she hear the babbling and screaming down the hall? Miss Larkly smiled broadly and told me that if I had changed a baby I would know what to do, only these were ten times heavier.

'But are they all right? Do they always make those sounds?'

Miss Weibe was opening a cupboard with a small key. 'That is the children's way of communication. It is nothing to be concerned about,' she said primly. I wondered if she had seen the 'Snake Pit'. I had, and if I'd known I was going to take a role in it.... Well!

The senior nurse was all in white and the junior nurse wore a uniform the same as mine but her shoes and stockings were white and I asked her why she wore the tails of her bib on the outside. She told me, proudly, that she was a second-year nurse. As she spoke she pulled another chair to the table and I was handed a pestle and mortar. I was to crush the pills.

The two nurses were intent on their task and I stole glances at them as we worked. Miss Weibe was a young woman no older than twenty-one or two, I thought. Her fair hair was pulled severely back and her cap stood up like a coronet. She was what I imagined a nurse should look like, squeaky clean, straight-backed and professional. Only a trace of lipstick showed.

Miss Larkly looked sixteen. She could have been eighteen. A nurse's cap was somewhere in her tumble of red hair and she had freckles. She handed me a soft white apron when we were finished preparing the medications and she suggested I wore it to keep my uniform clean. I was scared to ask how it would get dirty!

Miss Larkly bounced into the hallway on the balls of her feet looking as if she was off to play volley-ball, not to the dreaded ward where the noises now were loud, sounding as if half the patients were throwing up and the other half were so mad they were climbing the walls. Miss Weibe had stayed to lock the pills behind the cupboard door and then she joined us, tying the strings of her over-apron with a businesslike tug.

We were pulling a cart and stopped at a door marked 'Linen'. 'We fill this cart with bedsheets, etc., and jackets,'

Miss Weibe told me and clicked her tongue at the state of the shelves. Miss Larkly found a pocket-book hidden and hid it again while the head nurse's back was turned, winking at me as she did so.

We pushed the cart on to a door marked 'Laundry' and took another cart and filled that with towels and facecloths. The bowls set in the ledges were filled with warm water with soap beside them.

'All set,' Miss Weibe told me, and we went into the ward. The odour was strong from the beds. I tried breathing shallow and my head spun. Miss Weibe looked around smiling at the strange moon-shaped faces and called a welcome, until she saw Betina. She hurried to a bedside, snatching at a facecloth as she went. 'No, no, Betina. You must not put dirty b.m. in your mouth!' She pulled the girl's hand away from her face and wiped it. I had reached a far window and breathed in the night air deeply. I went back to help lift the patients from their soiled gowns, apologizing for my weakness.

'It's quite understandable first time. Some come in and faint before they've changed a bed,' Miss Weibe said seriously, shaking her head as if she couldn't understand it.

We continued down the row of beds. Miss Weibe removed the offending linen deftly and made the beds with mitred corners that she could have defied anyone to inspect. Miss Larkly pushed the soiled gowns into the bag with a screwed-up mouth, working quickly to get the job done but stopping to make a patient laugh while Miss Weibe shook on powder and inspected for bed sores.

I learned quickly that a jacket was a strait-jacket and I had to put a towel at the neck so it wouldn't rub. The straps that tied down the wrists and ankles of some of the overactive patients were to prevent them from hurting themselves.

It took three of us to lift up one large child-woman and change her, for she grasped us in a death grip as we moved her. Miss Larkly, who had the strong arms and sturdy legs a nurse needed, held her firm. Miss Weibe did the necessary down below, firmly and quickly, using terms like 'incontinent' and 'stools' and talking laxatives. Miss Larkly gritted her teeth, determined not to be strangled, while I handed the powder and pushed the sheets away.

I moved on to the next bed as they finally quietened the woman and I looked down into a large pair of violet eyes. I had never seen anyone with violet eyes before, they were ringed with dark lashes. The girl was a teenager and I felt a lump in my throat at seeing the exquisite face and the thin useless arms and body.

'This is Diane. Isn't she sweet?' Miss Weibe pushed back dark curls. She was obviously her favourite. The deep violet eyes were staring at me as if she wanted to talk. I said, 'Hello, Diane,' hoping she could.

'Diane doesn't speak but she likes us to talk to her. I think she knows what we are saying and everything that is happening. She is truly one of God's special children.'

In addition to feeling revulsion at the sights and smells of these twisted, misshapen bodies, I couldn't stop myself from questioning the ethics of letting these human vegetables exist. 'I would have thought her one of God's mistakes,' I said bluntly. Miss Weibe looked up, shocked at my statement, then remembering I was new there she shook her head, looking dedicated.

'No. It's a human mistake, don't you think, and as nurses it is our duty to do all we can for them. Would you take the laundry to the back stairs please, then we can start the bundles.' She dismissed me, eager to get to the next task.

I had to take the laundry to the back stairs through another ward filled with patients, and young nurses, silent as wraiths, floated by. I pushed the squeaky cart quickly, wanting to get back to familiar territory.

'Nurse,' a voice called softly. She called again and I turned to see if it was I who was being paged. I had never been called a nurse. I too could make a hospital bed and mitre the corners but I hadn't thought of myself as a nurse! A nurse in white approached me and said, 'Nurse' again, with a hiss in her voice. 'You are making a dreadful noise with that cart. Patients are trying to sleep. Please try and be quieter, and do something about that squeak!'

I nodded. I hadn't thought of the noise bothering these type of patients. I blushed. A girl half my age had pointed out the obvious fact that I lacked compassion. Chastened by this humbling bit of self-knowledge, I pushed the cart slowly and when I returned to the laundry I put vaseline inside the wheels for that was all I could find and I didn't like to go and ask Miss Weibe for a can of oil as if it was a garage.

We bundled clothes and readied the bathroom for the first bathings of the day. There was a list of names on the wall and the young nurse told me that each shift bathed a rota of patients so each one got a real soak every day. Then she went on to tell me how her days off were coming up and she played on the nurses' baseball team and they were going to beat the male nurses for sure. When we finished she said it was time for coffee and Miss Weibe went next 'so let's hurry!'

I didn't think I could look at food again. The smell of soiled bodies clung to the air and, I felt, also to me, but in the staff-room we lathered our hands and tidied our hair. Miss Larkly looked pink-cheeked and said she was just starving. Her hair still had a tumbled look as if she had just finished a glorious hike through the heather. We sat round a table with other nurses at their coffee break all talking at once and passing sandwiches and the cream and sugar. The coffee was steaming and smelled wonderful after the ward and suddenly I was hungry. The sandwich was the best I had ever eaten. I ate one quickly, listening to the chatter around me. A stout nurse, her cap loose and slipping over one eye, grinned at me. 'This is your first night, isn't it? Bet you feel you earned that sandwich.'

'Gosh, yes. May I have another one?'

'Sure can,' she pushed the plate towards me. 'The kitchen staff know we are all growing girls and make plenty.'

'I didn't think I'd ever enjoy eating again. I don't know how you stand it. Have you been over here long?'

'We all have to work over here often. Part of the training. It's where most of the treatments are done. Ah, 'tis a noble occupation.'

A flashy nurse at the other end lit up a cigarette and laughed. 'B.S.', she said emphatically. 'It's the money we're after.'

'Well, if that is so,' the stout nurse answered, pushing her cap further over one eye like a dough-boy and winking, 'I am told there are far easier ways of earning a living, and they say it's better money.'

The stout nurse went and filled her cup again and the young nurses, chattering like schoolgirls in a dorm, made our fifteen minutes disappear. Miss Larkly, who had grown pinker at the mention of boys, looked at her watch and we both hurried back to the ward.

The bathing routine went smoothly. Miss Weibe wheeled the patients in while I and Miss Larkly lifted them into the water, letting each one splash and play before we lifted them out. Then, as if they were large cumbersome babies, we dried and powdered them. After the last patient left we removed our rubber aprons and stretched our aching backs while Miss Weibe checked the bath mats, worried over the two large girls who had nearly slipped, and said we had done well and that bath routine had gone very smoothly with the obstreperous patients not trying to drown themselves or us. Miss Larkly had the credit for this for she had a firm, patient manner. I smiled at them. What did people mean, saying that young people were wild and lazy, sloppy and thoughtless? Then let them come here and see *these* young people. Gosh, I wanted to say, tired as I felt, 'You girls are smashing!'

But a chink in Miss Weibe's armour was showing, and it softened her. Wisps of hair had escaped her cap and she didn't put them back. She covered her face quickly to hide a yawn. We were looking out of the window. She had opened it wide to air the office. 'Won't it be great to be out there. Going to be a nice day.' I agreed. After the night I had never witnessed a more beautiful pristine morning. But then, after so many soiled beds and bottoms I had been cleaning, a cow's rump would have been beautiful this morning. Miss Larkly made no bones about it and said she was going home to have a bath and sleep for ten hours.

The patients' breakfast trolley arrived and Miss Weibe showed me how to encourage the patients to eat by pushing the food well on the tongue. 'And it helps to speak to them and make chewing noises,' she said, making mincing little movements with her mouth, only to have a patient spit on her bib. Miss Weibe pursed her lips as if she was about to say something, but checked herself.

The last straw came when we made one last round to be sure the patients were clean. The trolleys were removed and the office tidied for the on-coming day staff.

'Perhaps they are clean. They were yesterday,' Miss Larkly said hopefully, leading the way.

Like a flower, Miss Weibe had wilted. 'I suppose we should check first before we get any linen,' she said tiredly. The offensive odour hit us as we entered the ward. Betina was at it again and a stricken cry had escaped Miss Weibe's lips. Miss Larkly ran for a sheet and gown. Looking up to heaven, Miss Weibe squeaked, 'Jesus Christ, Oh Jesus Christ. There's more shit!'

FIFTEEN

AUCTION SALE

My days had no pattern. No longer did I hurry up so I could fetch kindling to get the fire going for breakfast, or call the goats from the bush, telling the children about the fine patch of saskatoons I'd found, but it was an interlude, an intermission before the main theme. Now I drove home where Christopher was ready waiting and, as if we were competitors in a relay race, he would jump in the car and race back to town again.

It took co-operation. Christopher milked the cow and goats and fed the calves, then separated the milk and had to be finished before I arrived; even the children, young as they were, understood it was part of the scheme. Dicky helped Peter get ready for school and Susy played quietly with Robin John, picking up after him and letting me rest, but I never really slept until Christopher came home. Then I would go to bed, until it was time to go to work again.

We didn't see much of each other, we were like ships passing in the night, buzzing each other in passing but keeping to our own course, and I discovered something. That mothers who go to work give their best to the family. I would have four days at home every two weeks, and it wasn't guilt that made me want to give all my time to them, bake cookies and find time to throw a ball. It was because I missed them.

After two weeks caring for the bed patients I was sent to the main building where the mildly retarded children lived. These girls and women could take care of themselves and many of them, if they didn't go to school, worked in various parts of the institution. Not many years later, The Manitoba School for Mentally Retarded, with 1,500 residents, was run under its new superintendent, Dr Glen Lowther and became one of the most advanced schools in North America. The girls that I had helped care for and who were behind lock and key were put in foster homes or were trained to work in the community, blending without difficulty into society.

I looked in awe at my first pay cheque. We were rich! Well it meant getting Betty back with us, that made us feel rich. Christopher walked her home on the end of a halter. It was a Sunday and we went to meet him, the children picking flowers on the way which I wove into a chain and placed around her neck. The other animals saw her coming down the lane. Eve mooed loudly and they stood washing each other's necks while the goats pulled off the flowers and ate them. Nine months later, for we had had Betty bred by A.I., she produced another heifer calf and her next calf was a sturdy bull that later became the herd sire. He gave us many daughters to grow into milking cows, which later became the herd.

We bought an electric stove and a few things for the house but we added no more improvements for we were already thinking of a new home, however far in the future it might be. We also went to a farm sale. Christopher had studied the newspaper and he read to me, 'There's a manure spreader, harrows, and listen to this. Two Jersey cows. Shall we go?'

'When is it?'

'Saturday. September 15th.' I consulted the calendar. I lived by the calendar, with red circles around the days that I was home.

'I work Friday but home on Saturday for two days. What time does it start?'

'Not till 1.30 p.m. You could sleep in the morning, I'll be home.'

'Then let's go.'

I have never liked farm auction sales. There is something sad, a finality in seeing a family's belongings spread out for everyone to poke at and wonder how cheap they can get them for. When we arrived, there were cars already lined up both sides of the lane. We walked in and there were odds and ends piled on tables on the front lawn. I stayed behind to look. There were old lamps, odd plates and faded curtains in a box. Lot 34. In another box was a lemon squeezer. 'Home Sweet Home' burned on to a slab of wood. I picked up a mug with the faded face of King George V in his Coronation robes. I wondered who had bought the mug. Had a little girl bought it for her mother, who had told her about the King and Queen in England and how she had once seen them pass by, or did the wife buy it with the groceries and put it proudly on the mantel? Had a grandmother frowned when the husband facetiously called it 'The Royal Mug', for Victoria had moulded her to stern propriety and the British Empire stood for something in those days.

A small saucepan was under it. It was enamel and chipped, stained inside from warming milk. I wondered how many babies the insignificant little pan had done duty for, or had it warmed milk for a sick old man! Someone picked it up and said 'What junk!' and I wanted to say 'It isn't junk. I bet they would have been lost without that little saucepan on a cold winter's night.'

Holding Robin John's hand, who insisted on walking everywhere these days and felt very grown up, we went and found Christopher. He was standing close to a manure spreader. Dried dung was stuck to it but he was guarding it as if it was the crown jewels and watching anyone who came near it as if they might steal it away from him.

'It's just what we want,' he whispered, 'but I think there's some others after it so I'm staying close. Did you see the Jerseys?'

'No. I was looking at a saucepan.'

'Do you want a saucepan?'

'No, but it looked so sad.' I was going to continue, but he pulled me away to the barn saying he wanted to get back to the spreader, so hurry.

'They come from Alf Adam's herd, and I saw him here and he recommends them. One has her fourth calf in

November and the heifer has her second calf soon.'

We examined them together. They were sleek and firm-footed with straight udders and other niceties that Christopher pointed out to me. I thought they were quiet and gentle.

'I'll stay with the spreader and if I can't get close you bid for the cows. Don't go higher than one hundred and fifty.'

I dragged my feet and left him. I hadn't had much sleep, and the farm depressed me. Was this the result of a lifetime of hard work? A tumbledown barn and a frame house badly in need of fresh paint? I had seen the owner, old and bent, wandering from item to item like a visitor on his own land, being pushed aside by the crowd. The furniture on the lawn was shabby and I could see inside the house the cracked lino and faded wallpaper, though in the yard the farmer's new combine and tractor, a large International, were being auctioned. The farm was low-lying and, they said, had seen many crop failures, but the last two had been good years. I wondered what his wife thought of the machinery, but she would be old too and her generation hadn't come up with the thought that she didn't have to put up with the old washing machine. I was wishing Dee could have been with me. 'Baby,' she would have said, 'we've come a long way!'

I gripped Susy's hand and carried Robin John to the car and it was warm in the sun. I thought we would wait there a while, and soon we all were asleep. I woke with a start. I hoped I hadn't slept long. The crowds were still there. I covered the children and ran back to the barn where a boy was slipping a rope on the young Jersey. I went close to her and followed them out. The bidding started quickly and I couldn't see Christopher so I waved my hand for a bid of one hundred. The auctioneer smiled at me.

'Oh, a fine little Jersey for the lady. Do I hear one hundred and thirty?' The numbers ran off his tongue and I nodded again at one hundred and forty, and fifty.

'One hundred and fifty and I am giving this delightful young cow away. Look at all the milk you'll get from her. My word! Do I hear sixty?' He looked straight at me.

Christopher said not to go over a hundred and fifty. Another five wouldn't hurt. The cow was worth it. I'll stop there and let whoever it is bidding against me have her. I nodded my bid.

'That's more like it. Another five, five, five. Yes, five. One hundred and sixty. Any more bids?' I looked away.

'Going, going, gone. To the gentleman at the back there.'

The bidding was slower for the other cow and I pushed closer and bought her for one hundred and twenty-five dollars. I made my way out of the crowd and went to find Christopher. He was standing by the manure spreader.

'I bought it,' he told me. 'I saw you asleep in the car so I bid for the first cow. Had to pay another ten higher than I reckoned. Didn't get the other one, someone pushed ahead of me and I couldn't catch the auctioneer's eye. Hear it went for a hundred and twenty. Pity.'

'I bought her,' I told him. He looked so pleased I didn't mention the first cow.

'Well I'll go and write a cheque and see about getting them home. I bought the harrows too, by the way.'

The boys went back to the car ahead of me and I stopped at the barn to see the cows we had bought. The owner was there, putting straw under them and stroking the old cow. I told him we had bought them and I asked him if they had names and he said they hadn't named them but just called them young cow and old cow.

'Have you farmed here long?' I asked him. He rubbed the stubble of his chin.

'Thirty-five years. Got no one to take it over so retiring to town.'

'You'll be able to take life easy now.'

'I've never taken a holiday so don't know nothing about taking things easy.' He turned and pulled over some hay and I left him, sorry for an old man who had known only hard work and wouldn't know how to enjoy his retirement.

Women were carrying boxes from the garden and the farmer's wife was standing at the kitchen door. She lifted her hand, I thought to brush away a tear or perhaps it was the prairie dust blowing in her eyes. I hurried to the car. I hoped we wouldn't have to go to another auction sale.

We went by the farm a few years later. The barn had collapsed and the house was a shell. There were grain bins in the yard. A company had taken over the land. The farmer had died within a year of moving to town and his wife, we heard, moved out of her daughter's place and bought a little house and they say it is very pretty and comfortable inside and she does a lot of entertaining.

SIXTEEN

CHRISTMAS IN OUR OWN HOUSE

It was starting to look like a farm. A small herd of Jerseys grazed in the meadow alongside the goats. The little hens still scratched in the straw and Tippy was showing off her five golden pups, as long-eared and pretty as her, for we had bred her to a fine male cocker. What was more, a tractor buzzed around the field harrowing in the manure the manure spreader had taken out.

Christopher was especially proud of the tractor. He had built it himself, buying two discarded John Deeres and making one good tractor out of them. He had given it a coat of green paint, with the help of the children, except Susy, who insisted on painting the tyres.

We had named the older cow Mrs Brown and the young one Tiny, and Mrs Brown had produced a bull calf, half Angus, that we would fatten. She now filled the pail so our cream cheque was larger. We had brought in the hay and bought alfalfa and straw, set for another winter, and I was offered another job.

We had continued our daytime–night-time existence for six months. I should have written verses about the many dawns, the daybreaks I witnessed. They didn't crash like thunder but peeked open shyly, as if to say, 'There, I told you it was going to be a nice day', or awoke stormy and cross as if the night had had a row with the stars. Christopher had never washed so many dishes or sorted as much wash, but we had coped and run the farm until I wondered if one of us would keel over. However, the prairies had tempered us well. We were too tough to fall, and to encourage us we had found a house.

The one-storey bungalow was ten miles away, and had to be moved. We had wandered through it and thought that with some (it turned out to be many) renovations we could make it a comfortable home. The house was ours for five hundred dollars if we moved it within a month, so we gathered round the table thinking and planning how we could arrange it. Dicky and Peter said they would dig a basement for us and Susy said she would watch that Robin John didn't fall in. We thanked them and then Christopher suggested a plan that would take as much co-operation.

I had been offered a position in the school department at the institute, teaching dancing and speech. The salary would be much higher and I would work school hours. To make the farm autonomous and to buy the new home, we would both have to be bringing home a salary for a while yet. Christopher could work a night shift at the garage. We asked the children what they thought of that plan. They had helped us decide where the bathroom would go and the basement that would have a playroom, and they nodded their heads wisely, Robin John copying every move. Dicky said they would dig very quietly when dad was asleep. So it was arranged.

The bank smiled generously upon us this time and soon the bulldozer came and dug out a basement, behind the log house and among the trees that we wanted to stay near. The blade went only four feet deep for the water table was high, and when the walls were built the basement stood high above ground level, but that would be earthed up later. We watched excitedly the big tow truck bringing our house down the lane, the men cutting back branches to let it through. Men whose business it was moving houses eased the bungalow on to the basement, guiding it one way and the other until it was a perfect fit.

We didn't move in right away. We first had a furnace put in and a bathroom. The kitchen floor had to be repaired and tiled, the hot-water tank installed and also the sewage pipes. I painted the living-room and sewed curtains and helped tile the bathroom. Christopher, and Jack Stewart, who owned the feed-mill and who had supplied us with pig meal and oats, and had waited so patiently for us to pay him, now helped us again and patiently laid new floor-boards and helped us find the place to put the basement stairs. We moved in just before Christmas.

It was our first Christmas in a home of our own. Our first good Christmas. I was especially glad we lived on a farm and doing the time-honoured things—milking the cows and putting the hay with its good honest smell in the mangers, bedding the cows down in deep straw. Outside the snow was crisp and our breath came in puffs. It was good to hurry in to the warm house knowing the animals were sheltered and content however cold the night.

I did something that Christmas that I won't do again. It was close to midnight on Christmas Eve and I had been busy all day, busy as a mother can get on that last day rushing to have everything ready. I iced the Christmas cake and made mince pies and a jelly salad and the children wrapped their gifts, a bit clumsily, and they yelled at each other 'stay out!' They were a long time getting to bed and to sleep. It was almost midnight. Christopher had fallen asleep in the chair. He had just crept around filling their stockings, hung at the end of the bed. I'd finished wrapping the last present, and the stuffing was ready to go in the turkey so I put on my coat and went outside.

It was cold, and the moon rode high. I looked up at the stars. They scattered stardust so deep I wanted to gather it up in my hands. I wondered which star had led the wise men, any would have been worthy. I walked on quietly, careful not to disturb anything. I was going to see if the cows really do kneel on Christmas Eve. Legend tells us they do. Thomas Hardy wrote about 'The Oxen', filling us with wonder. After all, they were there at the beginning, at the first Christmas. They know all about it. There is wisdom in their eyes, a wisdom of the ages. They are patient and giving and only ask for food and water and a warm barn. They repay us by always giving their milk, their calves, and finally their meat and their hide. They stand peaceful, calm, and look at us as if to say, 'Don't fuss, take it easy. Just do the best you can. There are warm days ahead. Shady trees and green grass, and at the end of it all "a quiet rest" and the nicest journey of all.' They are wise creatures.

I thought back to the sick heifer, another little Jersey, with a mealy muzzle and the kind of eyelashes a filmstar could envy. Then she was suddenly ill. The vet came and punctured her with needles and the latest cure and left us with pills and said keep her warm and hope for the best, but her eyes were dull and glazed and she lay still and she was dying.

Was it the medication, the care, the faithfulness, the spirit that made her want to live, to kick her heels to the sunshine and race to the meadow? I had crept down to her stall and in the doorway I saw her. She was kneeling. I stepped back, feeling I had intruded at a sacred moment. Then slowly she stood up and I entered and she took the soft hay and the warm gruel I offered her. She was going to live, and she had knelt to give thanks.

So knowing this, and that cows are said to kneel on Christmas Eve, kneeling to worship Jesus and to honour their ancestors who were there at the birth, I went to the barn door and lifted the latch. Suddenly my hand was stopped and I stood as if a voice had spoken. 'If you go into the barn you will wake the dogs! Tippy is in there with her pups, and Deena. You will disturb the cows. You will be an intruder and cows won't kneel if you stare. Do you have to have proof? What if the cows don't kneel? You will always be in doubt. You will even wonder if they ever did kneel!'

I dropped my hand and turned back. I was a silly woman and I was prying. Did I have such little faith that I had to steal down to watch? I pulled up my collar and pushed my hands into my parka pockets. What a bright, cold night it was, and how thankful I should be. We lived in a peaceful country and there was food for all. Our cows were deep in straw and our children snug in bed. Then I stopped. The cows' chains were rattling, one after the other; a little late came the last. That would be Betty. She is old, a little stiff. It must be midnight. They are kneeling. How could I ever have doubted them?

EPILOGUE—1967

'Open the gate someone, please.'

'You Robbie John, you're the nearest.' Dick prodded him.

'Why me? I opened the gate when we went out.'

'Hurry up. It won't hurt you to do it again.'

'It's not fair. I always have to open it.'

'I could have opened the gate six times while they were arguing,' Susan complained. Robin John got out of the car and stood at the gate, taking his time and kicking dust with his shoes.

'Then why didn't you?' I asked her.

'I think he has to learn to do things around here the same as I had to. I was opening gates before he was born,' she said airily.

'No you weren't,' I corrected her. 'We didn't have gates then.'

They helped carry in the groceries. Chrissy was hurrying up from the barn as fast as his little legs could carry him and Timothy, his seven-year-old brother, was behind him. I kissed my two younger children and Susan picked up Chrissy and hugged him.

'Sue, loo-pi-tubber-for-my-tat,' he said in her ear.

'Tim, what did he say?' Tim was the only one who could decipher Chrissy's baby talk.

'He wants his l-a-m-p-s-h-a-d-e,' Timothy spelled.

'Gee, you spell good.' Dicky patted him on the head. 'Where are my work pants, mom? I'll help dad until supper-time.'

'That's a good idea,' I told him. 'Peter has been down

there all day.'

'Well, I had these signs to make. I got paid for them today and I can't do everything.'

'My best-tat-Sue. Detit.' Chrissy beat his fists on the cupboard.

'Mom, what's for supper? I'll get it started.'

Christopher cried loudly.

'Will someone please give Christopher his hat so we can have less noise around here.'

'You're not letting that child go around with that thing on his head,' Dicky exclaimed. 'He looks crazy.'

'Oh, be quiet. I don't see anything wrong with him wearing a lampshade. He's only a little boy.' I defended him for peace and quiet more than any other reason. Little Christopher had grown a passion for strange headwear. He had just tired of wearing a tea cosy Grandma had sent us. That did look like a toque except for his ears that stuck out of the holes, but he had found the lampshade and now took to wearing it everywhere.

'I think we should discourage him, mother,' Susan added. 'He does look queer. I don't know what people will think!'

'Don't wear it Chrissy, you're embarrassing Susy. Her boyfriend Larry might see him,' Dicky teased, but Chrissy, smiling now, toddled out holding it on tight.

The usual commotion when anyone arrived home finally settled down and city sounds were forgotten as country sounds took over, soft and muted. They worked their balm, and peace reigned. Only the cry of the new calf could be heard, strained and pathetic, and the Baltimore orioles who had just arrived back to their tree and were singing the news. I looked out to see if they were still working by the barn. Georgie-gal was in the way. She had come to see her calf, mooing deeply, and the other Jerseys were standing behind her in sympathy.

I put my hand in the drawer for the paring knife and pulled it out with a scream. It was the squirrel again. I kept forgetting he made that drawer his home. They had to take him to the bushes further away, I decided. Who ever heard of keeping a squirrel in a drawer? He was a friendly little animal. Peter had rescued him from the dogs in the corner of the barn and he had been a pet from then on. His favourite place was on someone's shoulder. I had (without telling anyone) often given him his freedom, but so far he had perched on a tree by the back door and waited to jump on the first head that appeared (which was rather disturbing to visitors). I gave him a slice of apple and watched him turn it round in his front paws, using them like small hands.

I thought of all the things I had to do in the next few days. I wanted the house and garden to look especially tidy for our visitors, who were arriving from England. They were bringing direct news of families and taking a first-hand report of us back to them. I would weed the garden, mow the front lawn, wash the kitchen curtains, and what else? Have to do something about 'squirrel' and the lampshade. Maybe a cowboy hat would take its place, but he was pretty loyal to his 'hats'. They would think us a bunch of kooks. Our families were never quite sure about us. They had followed our adventures and struggles in Canada as if it were a serial story. They were always poised ready with a reply such as 'I told you so' and 'You wouldn't listen to us!' When I told them that our new house was coming down the road to us and would be fitted on to the basement, they said, 'Whatever kind of house would go along a road, and wouldn't the bricks fall loose?' And, when I told them we had built a new barn and we were milking twenty cows and raising a lot of calves, they said, 'And when are you going to stop having babies?' It was the 'eternal squelch'! So I did want our English visitors to return with a good impression of us. Photographs rarely did us justice.

When we had made a lawn around the house, fenced it in and I had flowers growing, I photographed Timothy, who looked lovable with his face washed, exploring a flower. But the house appeared askew. Tim was by then screaming at a bee and the dog appeared and scratched wildly in the background. If I took a photo of Christopher with a cow, he would never change his clothes. He hated being photographed and came out looking like 'Pa Kettle' at his worst.

Everyone tried to be nice, saying such things as, 'We are sure you will make a fortune one day and come home and see us with all those children'. It could be 'poor children' or 'dear children' considering how the story had been progressing. We had never implied that we wanted to make a fortune. Dairy farmers could hardly be called fortune-hunters.

The price of milk had gone up now we were selling fluid milk, with a bulk tank in the dairy, but we worked hard for our milk cheque. It was every day, without a break, summer and winter. The barn loomed darkly on a cold winter's morning and the pipes might be frozen and the cows slap you in the face with a wet tail and they have to be cleaned back before you can milk them. Calf milk has to be carried to the other shed and the young calves splash it down your leg in their eagerness and it freezes before you reach the barn again. They all have to be cleaned out and the tractor won't start. Try the handle and it kicks back in icy defiance, so you push manure through the snow, every unwieldly barrowful.

In summer the herd takes on a better look and you feel a moment's peace as they amble in, contented and sun-warmed, blossoms on their back and smelling of the woods, but it's a wistful moment. Cleo has had another bull calf. Kelly has sore feet and her milk is down. You hope Titch hasn't got mastitis and Dumpling's made another hole in the fence!

Yet we love this bit of Canada that we own. We love the small farm and the cows, although it is a strange love. We were too small to win, and lovingly, despairingly, we make frantic efforts to keep it going.

I hurried with supper. I wouldn't care what our visitors thought. We had done our best. It was a family farm and we wouldn't be wealthy but it was a good way of life. We knew the fundamentals and the family grew up on them. They knew that cows had to be cared for if they were to produce milk, that potatoes were apt to get bugs and that strawberries were back-aching to weed and worse to pick. It taught them to appreciate labour and never take things for granted.

No doubt our family will one day work or study in the city, but we hope the farm will have taught them reverence for life and a basis to judge things by.

The tractor was running and I saw Peter was sitting on it. I went out to see if he had remembered his medication. He didn't usually forget. He knew the pills enabled him to lead a more normal life, without the seizures. Peter went to Special Class and he had grown up knowing he wasn't as smart, that he was different, and it wasn't easy for him. He had suffered the cruelty of other children and he fell off bicycles and couldn't yet travel far on his own.

The countryside had changed. We had lost our leafy lane and there was a gravel road there now for the bus to travel along to take the children to town school. The country schools had closed and the roads were kept open all winter and life was easier, but we missed our leafy lane.

Perhaps we would one day see more of Canada, the mightiness of her mountains, the massiveness of her lakes, and we would again be challenged by them. We knew her prairies and the bush, the burning sand of summer and freezing cold of winter. We had endured it and accepted it. We had seen a new country grow. We feel we are part of its history. We have seen the people of the prairies, the people who got it started and the New Canadians who work to keep it thriving. We are part of it all. We are no longer the immigrants. We are Canadian, and that's something to be proud of.

ON GIANT'S SHOULDERS

by MARJORIE WALLACE *and* MICHAEL ROBSON

This extraordinary story of how three people fought against appalling odds is one of the most moving and heartwarming ever to be told. Leonard Wiles, an ex-lorry driver, badly wounded in the war, living in poverty but with a latent genius for engineering, marries Hazel.

Hazel is twenty years younger, married three times, born in a caravan, illiterate till the age of eighteen. Leonard and Hazel discover Terry, an illegitimate, abandoned, severly handicapped little boy. The story of this unlikely trio is the triumph of love, determination and skill over one of modern science's most tragic mistakes.

'A Dwarf on a Giant's shoulders sees further of the two.
George Herbert

0 552 10472 8—**65p**

YOU CAN GET THERE FROM HERE

by SHIRLEY MACLAINE

Starting her new book with the opening of her one-woman show in Las Vegas, Shirley MacLaine looks back over the past few years and tells the intimate story of herself and the fascinating world she lives in . . .

Persuaded into television by Sir Lew Grade, she made an enormously expensive series which was an instant disaster. From there she plunged into big-time politics, championing the cause of Senator George McGovern until his campaign ended in defeat—and disillusionment for his supporters.

Then came the journey to China, and experiences there which affected Shirley MacLaine more deeply than anything she had ever known. In that strange land, she began to see everything including herself, in a new light . . .

0 552 10411 6—**70p**

A SELECTED LIST OF AUTOBIOGRAPHIES AND BIOGRAPHIES PUBLISHED BY CORGI BOOKS